Don't Cry for Me, West Covina

Don't Cry For Me, West Covina is a delightful journey through the life and mind of Edward Guthmann. This affecting memoir is full of acute observations, celebrity insights, and a unique family history. Like a box of mixed chocolates where all the pieces are delicious."

David Leopold, author, *The Hirschfeld Century: Portrait of an Artist and His Age* and *Irving Berlin's Show Business: Broadway – Hollywood – America*

"He hooked me with the title — made me laugh out loud! — and then Edward Guthmann took me on a magical mystery tour of his life in *Don't Cry for Me, West Covina*. From his boyhood in a provincial Southern California suburb to his life as an ever-curious journalist, Guthmann enchants us with many an unexpected adventure and a cast of endearing and eccentric characters. He has a storyteller's gift, a humorous touch, and that finest of all qualities, a humane spirit."

Stephen Talbot, PBS documentary filmmaker, Peabody and Emmy award winner.

"Wry, wistful, occasionally eccentric, always eloquent — an absolute joy to read."

Ken Conner, journalist and author, *Westbound* and *Dying Words*

"Edward Guthmann's new memoir/collection of essays shares his lifelong passion for all forms of entertainment, sharing not just a family history but also an authorized peek at the notebook of a much-praised reporter and critic. Told with honesty and wit, a generous gift to be relished."

Leah Garchik, *San Francisco Chronicle* columnist and author, *San Francisco: The City's Sights and Secrets*

"Edward Guthmann's latest book is a delightful cornucopia of childhood memories and stories of what it takes to embark and succeed as a journalist and critic. One of Edward's great gifts is making his celebrities seem poignantly vulnerable and giving his ordinary folk a kind of glamour."

Charles Busch, actor; Tony-nominated playwright, *Tale of the Allergist's Wife;* and author, *Leading Lady: A Memoir of a Most Unusual Boy*

Don't Cry for Me, West Covina

Edward Guthmann

SHAFTER AVENUE PRESS · OAKLAND

Published by Shafter Avenue Press
5430 Shafter Avenue, Oakland, CA 94618

Printed in the United States of America

Book design by Ashley Ingram

ISBN 979-8-218-58020-9

for my nephew

Brian David Guthmann

Contents

Author's Note

This book is not your conventional memoir. The stories are arranged more or less chronologically but they weren't written in that order and they don't tell the whole story of my life. I simply wrote about the people, events, and places that interested me most and left the deepest memories.

Don't Cry For Me, West Covina began in December 2017 when I started contributing personal essays to *MyRetrospect*, a website where writers of the Baby Boom generation remember and reevaluate the 1950s, '60s and '70s. The majority of these 25 pieces first appeared there. They've been reconsidered, refined and in some cases expanded for this collection.

"Bobby Kennedy and the Year that Took Him" first appeared in the *San Francisco Chronicle* in June 1988. "Gregory Peck: A Man Who Lived Up to the Myth" made its debut in the *San Francisco Chronicle* in August 2003.

Parts of "Don't Cry for Me, West Covina," "Dad's Las Vegas, My Las Vegas" and "San Francisco: Working" appeared in my 2017 book *Wild Seed: Searching for My Brother Dan*.

"It Started with Fred Astaire," "San Francisco: A Dive in the Deep End," "I Ask a Lot of Questions," "I Like Dogs," and Epilogue are original to this book.

The names of certain individuals were changed out of respect for their privacy.

Don't Cry for Me, West Covina

916 Herald Street, our first house in West Covina.

Chapter One
Don't Cry for Me, West Covina

January 1, 1955. My father is watching the Rose Bowl on television. It's freezing in Chicago, but bright and glorious in Pasadena where Ohio State trounces USC. Everyone looks happy and healthy. "Wouldn't it be nice to raise these boys in California, where the sun shines all year long?" my dad asks my mother.

Dad is a doer, not a dreamer, and in three months he unloads his business, the Birchwood Garage, and sells the three-flat building where we live. Five Guthmanns squeeze into a station wagon—Davey is nine months old—and arrive in California on Dad's birthday, April 19. We don't know a soul in California and Dad doesn't have a job. He places a classified ad in the *Los Angeles Times* ("Seeking business opportunity in the automotive field, can pay cash money"), receives a huge stack of

Dad and Danny at the Western Auto store.

Danny, Davey, and Eddie. Newly arrived in California, summer 1955.

offers in the mail, and buys a Western Auto franchise in West Covina, 20 miles east of Los Angeles.

Dad finds us a three-bedroom, one-bath house at 916 Herald Street and pays $16,000. Our modest cul-de-sac has walnut trees and thirsty lawns, and we're surrounded by Baby Boom starter families with every reason to expect bright futures for their children. These are middle-class dads who fought in World War II, with names like Art and Joe and Frank and Maury. Moms wearing pedal pushers and Dinah Shore smiles, with names like Helen and Betty and Florence and Dixie. I go to kindergarten at Sunset School, my older brother Danny to Coronado School where his teacher is Mrs. Crabtree, the same name as the schoolteacher in *The Little Rascals*.

Winters are clear and gorgeous in West Covina, and on crisp January days there's a crown of snow on Mount Baldy. Summers are hot and dry, with sunshine so bright the colors bleach and flatten like an overexposed photograph. Butterflies, caterpillars, and grasshoppers abound. Ladybugs, pill bugs, the rare skunk or opossum. One day Dad kills a gopher by flushing it out of its hole with a garden hose and cleaving its neck with a swift, violent thrust of a shovel.

Few neighbors linger outside in the midday summer heat, but after dinner the Herald Street kids gather on the street and the grown-ups fan out to gossip and referee. Screen doors slam, a manual lawn mower calls out *kdop-kdop-kdop* and baseball games go on until the coppery twilight darkens and the ball can't be seen.

Herald Street briefly has its own celebrity when Betty Blakeney, who lives across the street from us with her truck-driver husband and three daughters, goes on the popular TV show *Queen for a Day*. *Queen* features four housewives on each episode and bestows big prizes on the one with the saddest hardluck tale. I heard someone say Betty has tuberculosis but, without understanding the gravity of the situation, I'm surprised when she goes on *Queen*.

Each contestant shares her story, after which the host Jack Bailey stands beside the applause meter and exhorts the studio audience to clap for their favorite. The more sorrowful the lament, the more tears shed, the likelier the housewife is to max-out the applause meter and get crowned. And—oh my God —Betty Blakeney wins! Draped in a sable-trimmed red velvet robe, bedecked

Queen for a Day

with a jeweled crown and holding a dozen long-stemmed red roses, Betty is seated like royalty on an upholstered throne. Her prize: a brand-new gas range with a griddle between the burners. Like every *Queen for a Day* winner, she cries.

Once a week the butter-colored Helm's Bakery truck motors down Herald Street. The Helms Man blows a whistle, parks mid-block, and onto the street swarm moms and kids to buy cookies, cakes, cinnamon rolls, and sticky, sugar-covered jelly doughnuts. The trucks are beautifully designed with ultra-long lacquered wooden drawers that slide out in back, releasing the delicious fragrance of fresh-baked bread.

My mom collects Blue Chip Stamps from the supermarket—I help her paste the stamps into fat collection books—and trades them at the redemption center for a lamp, end table, or portable TV. She orders clothes from the Sears catalog, and each year after Labor Day takes my brothers and me to J.C. Penney's for back-to-school shopping. For shoes we stop at Bud's Bootery, where the owner, Mr. Harris, measures my feet by sitting on a padded fitting stool and asking me to lift each foot onto the stool's slanted footrest. He unties and removes my old shoes, then laces up the two new pairs I try on: usually sneakers and leather dress shoes. After Mom pays the bill, Mr. Harris gives me a complimentary balloon that he inflates with an air pump attached to a foot pedal. He hands it to me with a smile and a pat on the shoulder. Nice man.

Where did all the Mr. Harrises go?

Like many Southern California towns, West Covina grows rapidly in the postwar years, its population exploding from 4,500 in 1950 to 50,000 in 1960. As a youngster I have nothing to compare it with, so I think my town is pretty cool. There's a movie theater, a bowling alley, a miniature golf course, and a public swimming

The Guthmann boys on Herald Street, 1958. I'm pushing the broom.

pool, the Covina Plunge, across the freeway. Once a month I walk to the liquor store to buy *TV Guide* for 15 cents and read about the upcoming installment of *Shirley Temple's Storybook,* then visit the Ranch Market on Vine Street where an enormous, top-loading cooler groans and sweats, dispensing ice-cold Nehi Grape, Hires Root Beer, and Royal Crown Cola in glass bottles.

Housing developments are everywhere, but in empty lots along their periphery you spot lizards, jackrabbits, or garter snakes. In the Walnut Creek Wash, a creek that runs half the length of town, kids catch polliwogs or swing Tarzan-style from a big rope into the water. Until, that is, the city brutally paves it over and leaves a massive concrete scar where our Huckleberry Finn fantasies bloomed. When I'm nine our family moves across town to Azusa Avenue, adjacent to one of the city's last remaining orange groves. My rowdy next-door-neighbor deputizes me in toppling the oil-burning smudge pots that growers use to protect trees from winter frost. That neighbor later became a cop.

In eighth or ninth grade, as the blinders of childhood start to lift, it dawns on me that West Covina—"the City of Beautiful Homes," according to its Chamber of Commerce campaign— is in fact homogeneous, culturally limited, and deeply conservative. I yearn to roam beyond the immediate radius of our town, to see a movie or a play in Los Angeles or Hollywood, but there's no rapid transit system in the Southland. Diversity? My grade school hasn't a single Black kid, just a handful of Mexican Americans and one or two Asians. In high school I can count six African Americans out of 2,200 students.

The congressional district representing West Covina is first in the nation to send a member of the ultra-right John Birch Society, John Rousselot, to the U.S. House of Representatives. At the town's only health food store, you can't purchase wheat germ or lecithin without the bellicose proprietor lecturing you on the encroaching Communist scourge.

And then, at thirteen, I discover *The World of Henry Orient* and my life is changed. The movie is set in New York City, where two preteen girls, Valerie and Marian, romp through Central Park, attend concerts at Carnegie Hall, and reside in cozy East Side brownstones. It affects me so powerfully that I vow to move to New York as soon as I'm able, there to soak up culture and become a new person. At the public library I study the *New York Times'* Arts & Leisure section to see what's opening on Broadway, marveling at the variety of dance, classical music, opera, and foreign films.

My New York fantasy lasts through eighth grade and four years of high school, so vividly that I draw floor plans for the brownstone I plan to buy on a leafy Manhattan street. There isn't anything to keep me in West Covina at this point: its politics and uniformity alienate me, and when I'm a high school junior and the campus newspaper polls students on their favored candidate for governor, I'm not surprised that Ronald Reagan wins two-thirds of the vote against Democratic incumbent Edmund G. "Pat" Brown.

———◆———

In fact, I never moved to New York. I settled in the San Francisco Bay Area, where I still live, but starting in 1975 I made one or two trips per year to New York and came to regard Manhattan as a second home.

I used to mock West Covina and take a dim view of people who never moved away like I did. I've shed most of that snobbery and realize now that my bias was the function of an overcompensating ego—a way to congratulate myself for being cooler than the Southland rubes. I don't know that you can divide communities and regions into Enlightened and Backward. We all occupy the same information universe, with the same access to facts and opinions, politics and culture. People can surprise you; you can't reduce anyone to their zip code.

West Covina changed enormously after I left in 1968. It's racially diverse now, with Latinos constituting 53 percent of the population, Asians 25 percent. The horrible smog of the 1960s and '70s is reduced thanks to auto-emissions standards, and a light-rail train connects residents to downtown Los Angeles.

When I look back, a lot of my memories are coated in a sweet, faint nostalgia, particularly for friends, neighbors, and schoolteachers who are long gone. And when I make a rare visit or watch *My Crazy Ex-Girlfriend*, a TV sitcom set in contemporary West Covina, I recognize almost nothing. My West Covina is a vapor, a dream. It exists only inside me.

The phenomenal Fred Astaire, with Ginger Rogers in *Top Hat*.

Chapter Two
It Started With Fred Astaire

When I was a kid in the 1950s, you could watch old movies on television all day long. Hollywood studios didn't know the value of their back catalogue—the concept of "vintage" or "classic" movies was yet to come—which meant that Los Angeles local TV stations could lease those titles for cheap.

That's how I found *A Damsel in Distress*, the 1937 picture that introduced me to Fred Astaire. It's a simple plot: an American entertainer in London (Astaire) romances a shy aristocrat (Joan Fontaine), sings splendid Gershwin tunes ("Foggy Day," "Nice Work If You Can Get It"), and dances brilliantly in a funhouse sequence that won an Oscar for choreography.

Movies repeated a lot on Los Angeles television, and I watched *Damsel in Distress* until I knew it by heart. Soon I was on to more Astaire movies like *Flying Down to Rio*, the 1933 musical that introduced Fred and Ginger Rogers as a dancing team. They were supporting players at first, billed below Dolores Del Rio, but they caught on quickly and eventually made ten pictures together.

Ginger was a very good dancer but Fred was transcendent, a breed unto himself. With Ginger you can see the effort in complicated numbers—her brow furrows, her shoulders hunch slightly—whereas Fred is rhythm, poetry, magic. A legendary perfectionist, he rehearsed each dance number several weeks in advance of shooting and insisted that each number be filmed with a minimum of cuts, showing himself and Ginger in full frame with their legs and feet always visible. For *Swing Time,* Fred's complicated "Never Gonna Dance" sequence required forty-seven takes. Somehow he made it look easy: the elaborate steps issue from his body as naturally and gracefully as flight from a hawk.

Fred Astaire opened the cinematic door for me, and by the time I was six or seven I was movie-crazy. I watched movies, read about movies, fantasized acting in movies. I idolized the stars and saw so many old pictures that I knew dozens of Hollywood character actors by name, like Zasu Pitts, Gabby Hayes, Edward Everett Horton and Marjorie Main. I read the lists of past Oscar winners in the *Information Please Almanac* until I knew each Best Picture winner and each acting honoree going back to 1928. I still do.

The magic of movies enraptured me as a child, but they were more than entertainment to me. They were comfort and escape, a world in which I was cushioned from family tensions, growing pains and the narrow parameters of acceptability that defined American life in the 1950s and '60s. Movies were my friend.

My parents didn't take us out to movies a lot, but I remember seeing Disney's *Lady and the Tramp* from the back seat of our station wagon at the Edgewood Drive-In. At home, I watched movies on our clunky, black-and-white console TV. Sitting on the living room rug, I delighted in Carmen Miranda, "the Brazilian Bombshell," with her snapping eyes and hats of piled-high fruit; Errol Flynn and Basil Rathbone and their elegant swordplay in *Captain Blood;* the comic team Olsen and Johnson in the loony farce *Hellzapoppin!*; and Gene Kelly, Hollywood's other supreme dancer, in *Anchors Aweigh.* I was hooked.

Margaret Hamilton in The Wizard of Oz, with Judy Garland.

The Wizard of Oz showed once a year on network television, and that was the highlight of the year for me, bar none. I loved the Hero's Journey that Dorothy takes from Munchkinland to Emerald City and back to Kansas. Loved the warmth and sincerity of Judy Garland, who transmits Dorothy's yearnings so palpably that you experience them in tandem with her. Adored Bert Lahr's Cowardly Lion and his deft delivery of E.Y. Harburg's lyrics ("Each rabbit would show respect to me, the chipmunks genuflect to me"); and Margaret Hamilton's riveting, go-for-broke turn as the Wicked Witch of the West. Ms. Hamilton inspired me to dress as a witch for Halloween when I was seven or eight. I still think her performance in *Oz* is one of the great achievements of Hollywood's Golden Era.

We didn't have VCRs, DVRs, cable TV or streaming back then, and movies played with frequent commercial interruptions. You'd get eight or ten minutes of movie at a time, bracketed by chirpy ads for Brylcreem hair gel ("A little dab'll do ya"), Maxwell House coffee ("Good to the last drop") or Alka-Seltzer ("Relief is just a swallow away!"). I didn't mind the commercials: watching that way was all I knew, and they had a familiarity and kitschy appeal. I wasn't bothered, either, by seeing black-and-white images instead of color, or by the truncating 3:4 aspect ratio of old cathode-ray TV picture tubes. I had no other point of reference.

My mother was critical of my fixation, and during summer afternoons when I'd watch countless movies she'd urge me to go outside and play like other kids. I had friends on the cul-de-sac where we lived, but I was basically a loner. One day she picked up the telephone, dialed the number of one of my Cub Scout friends, and stood with the receiver stretched out toward me. "You march right over here and ask Steve if you can come over to his house and play!"

At seven, I went alone to a movie theater for the first time. *The Light in the Forest,* starring James MacArthur as a white boy raised by American Indians before the Revolutionary War, was playing. No one would permit a seven-year-old to go unattended to a movie today, but in 1958 parents didn't need to be as vigilant. My mother dropped me off, and I nervously bought a ticket and ventured inside. Movie theaters had ushers then, patrolling the aisles with flashlights and monitoring the rowdier kids, and on this day a man kindly escorted me to the balcony and found me a single seat to the right of the projection booth.

Later, I acquired a comrade in arms when my younger brother Dave became a movie nut, too. *The Million Dollar Movie* was a staple on local TV channel KHJ, showing the same picture five days a week and four times over the weekend. If we found a movie we liked, we'd watch it over and over. We feasted on *King Kong, Godzilla, The High and the Mighty, The Adventures of Tom Sawyer, Buck Privates Come Home* and Charles Laughton's Quasimodo in *The Hunchback of Notre Dame*. On weekends and summer afternoons, Dave and I caught matinees at the air-cooled Eastland or Capri theater. We weren't discriminating: we'd see *Beach Party* movies, Bob Hope movies, Jerry Lewis movies, even horrible junk like *Atlantis, the Lost Continent*. Admission for kids was 35 cents; candy bars cost 6 or 12 cents.

Dave also got hooked on the Oscars and joined me in an annual predictions challenge. On scrap paper we'd create ballots for each category and rank nominees according to their likelihood of winning (five points for your first choice, four points for your second...). I often won, but Dave cleaned up the year Peter Ustinov won best supporting actor for *Topkapi* (1964). I'd ranked Ustinov the least likely winner, and Dave had him at number one.

We still make predictions each year. Dave is a statistician by profession, so he's deft at collecting and analyzing data, weighing variables and past Oscar trends. My approach is more instinctual. I don't think either of us expected a financial benefit from our Oscars fandom, but that's what eventually happened: My Oscar prognostications were an annual feature in the *San Francisco Chronicle* during my years as a writer/movie critic there, and Dave still wins cash prizes in the handicapping competitions he enters each year.

On rare occasions our whole family ventured off to a first-run cinema in Hollywood or Beverly Hills, an hour's drive from West Covina. Back then, blockbusters like *Ben-Hur, Cleopatra,*

Peter O'Toole as Lawrence of Arabia.

and *Mutiny on the Bounty* were given exclusive "roadshow engagements" at the Egyptian or Pantages on Hollywood Boulevard before fanning out to the suburbs several months or a year later. You paid a premium for roadshow runs and got reserved seats, same as with live theater. At twelve, I was thrilled when my dad took us to *Lawrence of Arabia* at the Stanley-Warner Theatre on Wilshire Boulevard. That movie's spectacular images, Maurice Jarre's bracing score, and the wily panache of Peter O'Toole as T.E. Lawrence are seared into me deeply. I still love *Lawrence* and have seen it several times in 70mm at the historic Castro Theatre in San Francisco. The overture starts and my breath quickens. I hear the thundering kettle drums, the crash of cymbals and the oceanic uplift of strings. I vibrate with excitement, down to my toes. Gets me every time.

I sometimes wish I could retrieve the wonder and surrender I felt watching movies as a child. That's why, when people ask me to name my favorite movies, I have two answers: first, the movies I loved most in my childhood, when my critical eye was undeveloped and my immersion pure and complete; and second, the films I revere today, many of which, like *Lawrence*, I've watched repeatedly. I love how my relationship to movies keeps evolving.

With age, you develop insight, perspective and, with any luck, empathy. The movies you discovered long ago become deeper experiences.

The Guthmann boys with our very own aluminum Christmas tree.

Chapter Three

Aluminum Christmas Tree

Until the year I turn ten, Christmas is a major highlight of my year. I'm such a Yuletide nut that one year, starting in July, I write letters to my aunts and uncles telling them what gift I hope to receive.

Everything feels special, charged about Christmas: the excitement in grade school when teachers serve punch and cupcakes on the last day before vacation; the storybook shimmer when neighbors string colored lights on their houses; when snowmen, built from tumbleweed that blows into town with the Santa Ana winds, magically appear on Southern California's front lawns.

In the Guthmann living room in West Covina, each year we have a fragrant Christmas tree, covered in tinsel and bedazzled with red, green, silver, and blue bulbs. A meager Santa Claus, fashioned from a hunk of cotton, stands on top instead of an angel—until, that is, a rat invades the box of Christmas decorations in the attic and lays waste to Santa.

By the end of each December, our tree has shed hundreds of needles on the living-room carpet, bringing no holiday cheer to my father. Each year he grouses about the mess, the cleanup, the bother of schlepping the tree to the curb on garbage day. Oy, did my father love to kvetch.

Finally, when I'm ten, Dad makes the unilateral decision to purchase an aluminum Christmas tree.

With an aluminum tree, he explains, "you buy it just once and save the cost of purchasing a new tree each Christmas. It could last five, ten years or more. Think of the money saved." At no point do notions of beauty, aesthetic pleasure, or the woodsy fragrance of pine needles enter the discussion. All such concerns are eclipsed by this object lesson in thrift.

Our Evergleam Stainless Aluminum Christmas Tree, which debuted at the American Toy Fair in March 1959, arrives in a large cardboard box. Each year, from fifth grade until I graduate from high school, the family gathers in the living room, where my brothers and I assemble the tree under my parents' supervision. There are three wooden posts coated in shiny silver paper that join to form the trunk. Branches come next: dozens of them individually wrapped in long, thin brown-paper sleeves and covered with hundreds of aluminum foil "needles."

Each branch is carefully removed from its brown-paper sleeve, lest the narrow strips of foil bend and wrinkle. Working from the top down, my brothers Dan, Dave, and I insert each branch into evenly spaced holes drilled into the trunk. Ornaments are next. No electric lights, please. "The tree can become charged with electricity from faulty lights," the Consumer Product Safety Commission warns when the first aluminum trees go on the market, "and a person touching a branch could be electrocuted."

The tree isn't finished yet. The pièce de résistance is the rotating color wheel that sits on the floor. A plastic disc attaches to the wheel, with kidney-shaped gels that project red, green, blue, and amber patterns onto the tree.

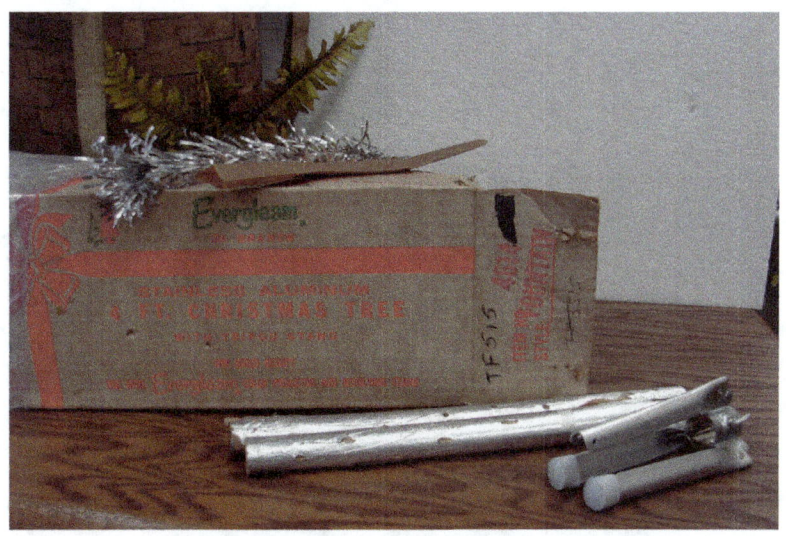

When the aluminum tree is brand-new to our living room, our family sits in a circle and stares at the finished tree. Andy Williams sings syrupy Christmas carols on the stereo. Stockings are hung. My parents choreograph this family tableau to imbue my brothers and me with the holiday spirit, it seems—to allow the aluminum tree to work its cunning magic.

But instead of awe and delight, we feel nothing. This artificial tree is cold, soulless.

It may be that hindsight sheds a coating of cynicism onto my tale—the feeling that the aluminum tree, as my brother Dave joked much later, was "a form of child abuse" that robbed us of a proper Christmas. But my recollection is that even then, my brothers and I thought it was kind of dumb.

It's significant that my story takes place in the early 1960s, when space-age design and anything futuristic gains cultural currency and *The Jetsons* becomes a huge hit on prime-time television. And really, what could be more "Jetsons" than an aluminum tree?

What could be more "Jetsons" than an aluminum Christmas tree?

Apparently, a lot of people agreed. Between 1959 and 1969, the Aluminum Specialty Company of Manitowoc, Wisconsin, produced more than one million aluminum Christmas trees. They retailed for $25 apiece—roughly $250 in today's economy.

Why would anyone spend so much? According to the Sears 1963 Christmas Book, the reasons were abundant: "Whether you decorate with blue or red balls, or use the tree without ornaments," Sears enthused, "this exquisite tree is sure to be the talk of your neighborhood. High-luster aluminum gives a dazzling brilliance. Shimmering silvery branches are swirled and tapered to a handsome realistic fullness...It's really durable. You can use it year after year."

I realize I've told this story at the expense of my father, who thought he'd done a wise and prudent thing by buying an aluminum tree that would save us money over time; and maybe at the expense of my mother, who may have hated the tree but kept quiet in order to maintain peace in the household.

What I didn't appreciate until much later was my dad's struggle to support a family of five with the income from his Western Auto store. Western Auto was a national chain and its stores were junior-size versions of Sears: auto parts, electrical and plumbing, bicycles, toys, furniture. The profit margin was small, meaning that Dad's decision to bring a fake tree into our house — and have us reconstruct it annually for the next decade — wasn't driven by "Bah, humbug!" stinginess, but rather by financial necessity.

As the mid-1960s passed, the aluminum Christmas tree would fall out of favor in American homes, gathering dust in basements and attics or selling at yard sales for as little as 25 cents. *A Charlie Brown Christmas* contributed significantly to its demise. You may remember Charlie and Linus encountering a window display of aluminum trees in that 1965 television classic and turning away in disgust. Charlie instead chooses a small, scrawny sapling—symbolically casting his vote for authenticity over tacky commercialism.

In 1970, my father would unload the Western Auto store and open a bicycle store, which proved to be the biggest financial success of his life. The timing was perfect: with the energy crunch of the early '70s and the push toward fitness among adults, suddenly people of all ages were riding bicycles in suburban Southern California.

I'd like to report that once the business took off and Dad's nest was nicely feathered, he gladly took that damn aluminum tree, its individually wrapped branches and its rotating color wheel, and tossed the lot in the garbage. And then brought home a genuine, live Christmas tree.

But he never did. And my mother, presuming she even had a desire for one, never requested it. Neither of my parents was what you'd call aesthetically inclined, and neither lost the habit of parsimony they'd learned as children of the Depression.

That's almost the end of my story. Weirdly enough, the aluminum Christmas tree never disappeared altogether and in fact scored an unexpected comeback. In 2004 Wisconsin artists John Shimon and Julie Lindemann published the photography book *Season's Gleamings: The Art of the Aluminum Christmas Tree.* The following year, a rare seven-foot-tall pink aluminum Christmas tree sold online for $3,600. The trees even appeared in museum collections. Ah, the allure of retro kitsch.

Somewhere my late father, a true early adopter, is feeling proud of his foresight. And his thrift.

Sadie Kaufmann Guthmann on her wedding day, 1902.

Chapter Four

That's No Midget,
That's My Grandmother

I'm in the third grade riding home on the school bus. The sun is out and kids are making the usual racket when the bus passes a tiny old woman walking on the side of the road.

"Hey!" the boy in front of me shouts and points. "Look at the midget!"

"That's no midget," I say. "That's my grandmother."

True story. Grandma wasn't a midget, but she was very, very short. When she got married in 1902, she stood four-foot-ten and weighed ninety-two pounds. By the time I was growing up in the 1960s, she had shrunk and was probably four-foot-seven, four-foot-eight at the most.

Sadie Kaufmann was born in Chicago in 1878, the child of German Jewish immigrants Simon Kaufmann and Rebecca Lehman Kaufmann. Rutherford B. Hayes was president that year. Pancho Villa, Joseph Stalin, and George M. Cohan were also born in 1878. Tolstoy's *Anna Karenina* was published, and Thomas Edison patented the phonograph.

Every year, Grandma spends the winter with us in California to escape the frigid Chicago winters and the risk of falling on ice and breaking a hip. Even when I'm five or six, she seems ancient to me. Her skin is crepey, her walk slow and lopsided, and she is easily bewildered. Grandma doesn't talk much during her visits, because she is nearly deaf.

She wears a transistor hearing aid, which fits in a little sleeve that clips to her bra under her dress. A thin raggedy wire twists upward, connecting to a plug in her left ear. This primitive device is barely functional, probably five or ten percent as effective as hearing aids today. When she talks on the phone, she has to hold the receiver upside down with the earpiece against her bosom.

Given that Grandma hears so little—we have to yell for her to understand—my brothers and I interact with her very little. Her deafness isolates her, and although she doesn't complain, it's clear that it saddens and depresses her.

Even at the dinner table, where voices are close and she can read lips, Grandma doesn't speak much. Each night as we finish dinner my dad asks her if she's had enough to eat. And each night she gives the same reply—"Yes, I've had plenty"—and then adds a phrase in German: "*Sehr gut geschmeckt.*" It tasted good.

Kids are generally impatient and disrespectful with the elderly, and with Grandma my brothers and I are often terrible. In the mid-'60s Granny Goose Potato Chips runs a lot of TV ads, and since Grandma's wobbly gait resembles a duck or a goose, my brothers and I nickname her "Goose." Sometimes if she enters the living room,

The Guthmann family, 1917. Rosalyn, David R. Guthmann, Dave Jr., Grandma Sadie, Marvin.

we slowly chant the name with a low, elongated "G-o-o-o-se" that she can't hear. If a friend visits the house and doesn't know about Grandma's hearing, one of us will say in mock indignation, "Grandma, did you just fart?"—loud enough for everyone but Grandma to hear—and relish the friend's shocked reaction.

Oh, we were bad. Years earlier, when my little brother Davey was four or five, my parents went out and left Grandma to babysit the three of us. We exploited her slowness and poor hearing, her inability to catch us when we ran. At one point she was chasing Danny when Davey approached from behind and bopped her lightly on the head with a dictionary. Danny and I thought that was priceless.

Sadie K. Guthmann is a child of the late 19th century, and by the time I know her in the 1950s and '60s she feels displaced. "I don't belong in this world," she says. She can't understand young people's music or fashion, thinks it's unhealthy that I spend hours watching television in the afternoon when I could be outdoors playing ball like my dad did in his youth. Does she yearn for a simpler, quieter world? Do young people seem reckless and rude? No doubt.

Grandma has very little to keep her busy or engaged. She doesn't read much because the type in books and newspapers is too small. Most TV programs are "silly" to her, the big exception being *Family Affair* with Brian Keith as a bachelor uncle raising three orphans. She adores it. She has no friends she could visit or meet for lunch.

She wants to help my mother with dinner, but she's not steady on her feet. Mom feels sorry for her and asks her to dry the dishes, thinking it will help her feel useful—but Grandma's eyesight isn't good and the dishes get half-dried. The only things she ever cooks are matzo balls (dense and flavorless) and an apple-and-cinnamon pastry called Apple Charlotte (very sugary, not bad).

Mostly she naps and goes on walks. Once or twice a day Grandma dons a woven-straw sun hat that ties under her chin and then flattens into a half-moon when she takes it off. She wears a coat or a cardigan, heading off through the neighborhood in her lopsided, determined stride. She always wears a dress. Not once in her life has Grandma ever worn pants.

As she walks she issues a little tune of sorts, barely audible, that seems to establish a rhythm and propel her forward. It's the same soft, three-count whistle you hear as she walks through the house: "Phoo-phoo-phoo, phoo-phoo-phoo." Like the Little Engine That Could: *I think I can, I think I can.* Sometimes if she starts to stumble, she chuckles and says, "Look at me, I'm *shikhur*"—Yiddish for drunk.

During her three-month visits, Dad takes Grandma once or twice to temple for Friday night Shabbat services. She wears her girdle and stockings, her best knit dress, and heavy black old-lady shoes. She applies lipstick and rouge, brushes her wispy hair and corrals it in a hairnet. To complete the ensemble, she sometimes brings out her ancient fox-fur stole, its taxidermied head and legs still attached.

Grandma likes going to temple. She doesn't know anyone but given that she grew up with devout parents and volunteered at Temple Emanuel in Chicago, where she ran the ladies' sewing circle, she brightens at the opportunity to reconnect with tradition. She especially loves the music. Her hearing is terrible, but the liturgy is familiar enough that once she catches a few notes she jumps right in—singing louder than the rest of the congregation, two or three beats behind. People turn and glance with slight, indulgent smiles.

Only Dad knew Grandma when she was younger, when she raised three children in a series of modest Chicago flats; when she washed the family's laundry by hand ("That was a big event in our household when Mother got a washing machine"); when she baked the bread and created a dinner each night on the meager stipend my grandfather allowed.

"Mother never talks about Father anymore," Dad says one day, and seems saddened by it. My grandfa-

Grandma with my grandfather and my Uncle Dave, during or soon after World War II.

ther, who died in 1953 when I was two, is rarely mentioned by anyone and only much later do I get a sense of how my grandmother was dominated and underappreciated by him. He drank a lot, and according to Dad he would freely spend money at a neighborhood tavern while limiting Grandma's allowance: "He was so damn tight all the time. Mother wanted to do this or that and she had such a problem. He was always moaning or groaning."

I couldn't understand it at the time, but I lost a lot by having a grandmother who couldn't hear. I never really got to know her, which makes me sad, since she was the only grandparent alive as I was growing up. One year during her annual visit, I asked her questions about her early life, partly out of curiosity and partly because I sensed she'd appreciate the interest. I wish

My mother Roberta, Grandma, and our neighbor Betty Blakeney, 1957.

I'd recorded it, because all I remember is her saying she quit school after the eighth grade ("I was very foolish") and went to work for her father.

What else might I know if I'd taken more interest? How she met my grandfather? What Chicago was like for a young girl in the 1880s and 1890s, before the automobile? What kind of people her parents, Rebecca and Simon Kaufmann, were? What prejudice she encountered as a Jew?

Grandma died in 1972, four months shy of her ninety-fourth birthday. She was greatly diminished at the end and spent her last two years in a nursing facility near my parents. My mother visited her every day, and after a while Grandma believed Mom, her daughter-in-law, was in fact her daughter. "Roberta, how many children do you have?" she once asked. And every day the same plaintive question: "When am I going home?"

I have some letters Grandma wrote me when I was small and fortunately a wealth of photographs that my father and Aunt Rollie kept until they died. I'm grateful for them, but I wish I knew more of the stories that go with them.

Chapter Five

We Called It Junior High Back Then

The last time I'd seen Diane Weston she was six years old. I remembered a sweet smile, lustrous brown hair and the last vestiges of baby fat. She probably wore a plaid jumper, shiny black Mary Janes and white socks.

That was kindergarten. Diane and I were best friends that year but now, in my first week of seventh grade at Cameron Junior High, she's someone I barely recognize.

At twelve she's prematurely developed, a ripe Lolita with the self-possession of a young woman. When I pass Diane in the hallway, when our eyes meet in the cafeteria, she doesn't smile or say hello, even though I'm certain she remembers me.

I don't say hello, either. Six years are an eon in a child's life, and after a long gap when we attend different schools, make new friends and slide into the scary, sticky realm of early adolescence, we are total strangers. She's the head of a social clique to which I'm an outsider. Throughout seventh and eighth grade, and for that matter all of high school, too, we never speak to each other.

And yet I'm fascinated by Diane and her apparent fearlessness. Can a twelve-year-old girl swagger? Diane does. Gently swishing her hips, she walks down the hallway like preteen royalty, glancing from side to side to appreciate the effect she's having. She has big bright eyes and gorgeous full lips and wears V-necked sweaters that emphasize the contours of her breasts.

Diane in kindergarten.

Without question she is the most desired, most alluring girl in seventh grade—a source of power she enjoys.

Social hierarchies are quick to develop in junior high—it isn't called middle school until years later—and from day one Diane is queen bee. Girls copy her, lobby to be her friend. Boys stare and whisper. There's a patriotic song, "I Like It Here," that we all learn in Miss Booth's music appreciation class, and during recess Diane leads a rowdy claque of girls across the playground, loudly singing the anthem and mocking its cornball lyrics: "Lift my head to the sky and say how grateful am I! Yes, I like it he-e-re!"

A rumor circulates that Diane and a seventh-grade boy are already having sex. In 1962 the notion itself is scandalous. It's probably untrue, a fiction disseminated by girls who covet the attention Diane draws so easily to herself. True or not, the story is so tantalizing, and Diane such a provocative presence, that most of us enjoy believing it.

Unlike Diane, I'm a misfit. My teeth are crooked, I'm bad at sports, and the bullying that seventh- and eighth-grade boys exhibit with escalating magnitude is scary. It doesn't help that my homeroom teacher Mrs. Kiser is prone to picking class favorites, even flirting with the handsome, physically mature boys. I feel second-class.

One afternoon I'm at Von's supermarket with my mother. I kill time in the magazine section while she shops and meet her later at the front of the store, talking to a vaguely familiar, gray-haired woman. "Eddie, do you know who this is?" Mom asks. I don't. "This is Mrs. Weston, Diane's mother."

There's a careworn expression on Mrs. Weston's face. She doesn't say much in that short conversation, but I get the impression from her sad eyes that she's consumed with worry over her out-of-control daughter. She's much older than most moms —over fifty, I would guess—and the job of raising a willful, sexually mature preteen is more worrying, probably, than it would be for a younger mother. Looking back, I hope she had someone to talk to and didn't hold that anguish inside.

Junior high is a horror show for everyone, kids and parents alike, and I'm a captive participant. Kids are meaner, cliques more rigid, the pressure to conform unrelenting. Seventh grade is tough but eighth grade, when hormones ignite even higher and several teachers are masters of humiliation, is much worse. It's also the year JFK is killed. How many thirteen-year-olds have the wisdom or experience to process a jolt like that? Three months later the Beatles explode on *The Ed Sullivan Show*. They're a great band, but for teenagers in 1964 they're also a distraction from our awareness that something we assumed to be so basic—our faith in a safe and just America—is suddenly tenuous.

I started my story with Diane Weston and writing about her has made me think about her more than I have in 50 years. I can barely picture her in high school, but my West Covina friend April recalls that she hung out with the "hard" girls, the ones with teased-high hair, tight skirts, and lots of bugger-off cat-eye makeup. "She was very smart and kind of full of herself," April says, and after high school she became a "hard-core born-again Christian" and renounced her unruly ways.

And then what? I had no idea, but in the summer of 2024

Diane's niece announced on Facebook that Diane had died of Alzheimer's, and posted a photo of her at the end, looking lost and confused but still beautiful. I hope she made peace with her mother long ago. I mentioned that Diane seemed powerful and fearless in seventh grade, but I'm sure her story has deeper layers. Were there family conflicts, private sorrows and insecurities she masked with the brazen toss of her hair and forward thrust of her chest?

We all develop survival strategies in tough times. The bewildering years of junior high would be insupportable without them.

Chapter Six

"We've Got a Really Big Shew For You Tonight..."

In the years when I was growing up, which were the early years of television, my family watched a lot of TV together. There weren't a lot of choices, just three network channels and three local channels. We watched family sitcoms like *Leave It to Beaver, Father Knows Best,* and *My Three Sons,* and on many nights a variety show. Saturday you had Jackie Gleason. Tuesday, Red Skelton; Thursday, Dean Martin. And from 1948 to 1971, Sunday night belonged to Ed Sullivan.

Sullivan was the unlikeliest of TV hosts. Originally a syndicated newspaper columnist, he was devoid of charisma or performing talent. "Ed does nothing, but he does it better than anyone else on television," comic Alan King cracked. Comedians loved to lampoon his hunched posture, barracuda face and clenched speech. "We've got a really big *shew* for you tonight," he'd announce at the top of the hour.

He earned the nickname Old Stoneface, but he had a great eye for talent, and a keen sense of timing. "Who's hot right now? Who's *about* to be hot?" Ed always knew.

Today he's best remembered for introducing Elvis Presley and the Beatles to U.S. audiences, but in fact Sullivan booked the people you most wanted to see every week, year after year. Watching his show, you felt like a participant in a collective na-

The Beatles on *The Ed Sullivan Show*, 1964. *Express Newspapers/Hulton Archives via Getty Images.*

tional experience—like having your hand on the pulse of popular culture. Anyone with a hit record, anyone riding high with a Broadway smash went on Sullivan. His show offered variety in the fullest sense of the word. Singers, comics, Chinese acrobats. Plate spinners, sword swallowers, an Israeli violin prodigy. Certain acts caught on, like the anthropomorphic Italian mouse Topo Gigio ("Eddie, kiss me good ni-ight"). Same with Señor Wences, a marvelous Spanish ventriloquist who drew puppets on his fist with lipstick and introduced catchphrases like "Dee-fee-cult for you, easy for me."

Sullivan's tenure coincided with the Civil Rights era, and during that time he gave Black entertainers a visibility they'd long been denied. "And now, right here on this stage," he'd say, and bring on James Brown, gospel powerhouse Mahalia Jackson, Diana Ross and the Supremes; comics like Flip Wilson,

Richard Pryor, and Jackie "Moms" Mabley. He shook hands
with Nat "King" Cole when that was deemed controversial and
kissed Pearl Bailey on the cheek, angering Southern advertisers
and viewers. But Ed and his network weren't altogether fearless.
When the Rolling Stones guested, CBS's Standards and Practices office insisted they replace the lyric "Let's spend the night
together" with "Let's spend some time together"—a silly sani-
tizing gesture that Mick Jagger mocked by rolling his eyes.

I remember French chanteuse Edith Piaf making multiple
appearances, each time in a simple black dress delivering her tri-
umph-through-tears anthem "Milord," and Italian-American
singer Connie Francis, whose plaintive, kitschy sigh made you
think she would burst into tears. Each week Sullivan welcomed
stand-up comics, mostly Jewish: Jackie Mason, Myron Cohen,
Jack Carter, Totie Fields, and Joan Rivers. And, since the show
originated in Manhattan in the same theater where *Late Show
with Stephen Colbert* is taped today, you got the grit and moxie of
native New Yorkers. I'm thinking of Jerry Stiller, a Jew from the
Lower East Side, and Anne Meara, his Irish-American wife from
Long Island. Those pungent accents came right off the streets
and announced, indisputably, "I'm a New Yorker." Sadly, those
accents are disappearing today.

I grew up loving Broadway musicals, and I have Ed Sullivan
to thank for that. I remember Lucille Ball coming on to sing
"Hey, Look Me Over!" from her short-lived musical *Wildcat*,
and dazzling Gwen Verdon offering "If My Friends Could See
Me Now" from *Sweet Charity*. A spot on the Sullivan show
could rouse a sleeping box office, create a hit where an early
closing notice seemed imminent. In his memoir *On the Street
Where I Live, My Fair Lady* lyricist Alan Jay Lerner wrote that
when his show *Camelot* opened in 1960, "word-of-mouth was

not good and the chances of recovering the investment seemed infinitesimal." But when Sullivan observed the fifth anniversary of *My Fair Lady* with a full-hour tribute to Lerner and his songwriting partner Frederick Loewe, he offered to showcase four songs from *Camelot*. "Ed, one of the most gracious gentlemen in television, gave us carte blanche," Lerner wrote.

The following morning, Lerner was awakened by a phone call from the manager of the Majestic Theatre on West 44th Street: After weeks of sluggish box office, there was a line around the block. *Camelot* became a solid hit, won several Tonys and ran for two years. There were probably hundreds of stories like that. The Sullivan effect was so wide that a song in *Bye Bye Birdie*, "Hymn for a Sunday Evening," playfully satirized his influence. A teen-age girl from Sweet Apple, Ohio is about to make an appearance on the Sullivan Show, and her family is so overjoyed that they burst into song: "Ed Sull-i-van! Ed Sull-i-van! We-e-e're gonna be on Ed Sull-i-van!" At that time, Ed had the same level of clout and fame that Oprah enjoyed at her peak. Probably more.

Julie Andrews and Richard Burton in *Camelot*, 1960. An appearance with Sullivan turned their struggling show into an overnight hit.

At the same time, Sullivan was a controversial and sometimes abrasive figure. "As the show's producer, he took dictatorial control over every aspect of his production," wrote James Maguire in the biography *Impresario: The Life and Times of Ed Sullivan.* "In contrast to his persona as the reserved and respectful host, as producer he didn't care who he offended, with the exception of a very few high-profile guests." After a Sunday afternoon rehearsal, he would often cut or reshape a comic's material, assign a different song to a singer, or even drop a performer altogether if that person didn't "jibe with his gut instinct of what would reach the home audience."

During those years, *The Ed Sullivan Show* was watched each week by an estimated 75 million Americans. It was a Sunday night ritual in the life of my family. When I look back, it feels significant that we watched it in real time. Nobody had DVRs or TiVo or streaming then, so you couldn't record a show; you couldn't pause or rewind during a broadcast. You had to rush to the refrigerator for a snack during a commercial. You had to focus, unlike the multi-tasking, over-distracted TV audience of today. It made the experience of sharing that show—with your family, with the rest of America watching simultaneously —that much richer.

In March 1971, CBS foolishly decided to cancel *The Ed Sullivan Show* after 23 years and an astonishing 1,068 episodes. The network wanted to target the youth demographic with its greater potential ad revenue and saw the Sullivan audience as staid and irrelevant. Ed was irate at being axed and refused to host the additional three months of scheduled shows. The network ran reruns instead.

Television's ultimate impresario lived another three years beyond his cancellation, dying a few weeks after his seventy-third birthday on October 13, 1974. At St. Patrick's Cathedral in

Sullivan with the unhappily censored Mick Jagger. *Express Newspapers/Hulton Archives via Getty Images.*

New York, 3,000 people attended his funeral on a cold and rainy day, honoring a man whose personal manner was stodgy and uptight, but whose instincts as host and tastemaker brought us decades of great entertainment.

Chapter Seven
Good Morning, Mrs. Shafer

It takes a long time to learn gratitude. When I look back and recall some of my schoolteachers, I'm sorry I never took the time to thank them—to let them know their hard work and kindness made a positive impact that still reverberates through my life.

I wish, sometime before she died, I had located my third-grade teacher Shirley Shafer. Picture a vivid personality, bright-red hair, a clarion voice and take-charge personality. Mrs. Shafer was an East Coast Jew, a bit of a Shelley Winters or Bette Midler type—and therefore out of place in WASPy 1950s West Covina. She had moxie. She knew who she was.

I liked her very much: She was strong and outspoken, but warm and caring beneath the brass. At school we had something called the "freeze bell" that rang loudly at the end of recess, signaling students to stop talking, stand stock-still for fifteen seconds

Mrs. Shafer, my third-grade teacher.

and then walk—not run!— to their classrooms. One day a girl made her friend laugh out loud during the freeze and Mrs. Shafer, on playground duty that day, quickly admonished her. I didn't hear what the girl said but Mrs. Shafer fired back like a cannon: "Young lady, it's time you learn respect for your elders and superiors!" I was stunned by Mrs. Shafer's comeback and command of language. It felt like a scene from a movie.

Mrs. Shafer taught us penmanship and endeavored to foster a love for reading. One day she had us read a short biography of Abraham Lincoln and then summarize it in writing as a homework assignment. "Eddie, did you write this yourself?" she asked me the next day. "Yes," I answered, a bit puzzled by the question.

"Well, it's very good," Mrs. Shafer said. She was the first person to tell me I had writing talent. I remember how good that felt. Thank you, Mrs. Shafer.

Nine years later, I was a senior in high school and Virginia Browning was my English teacher. Quiet and conscientious, she was a totally different personality from Mrs. Shafer but similar in that she was a paragon of efficiency. Divorced, she was raising two teenage daughters while teaching five or six classes a day. I got the feeling she was lonely, probably deeply hurt by the end of her marriage.

I imagine Mrs. Browning going home to fix dinner each night for her daughters, asking how their day went and staying up late to grade papers and write lesson plans at the dinner table. The next morning she would dress quickly, fix breakfast and dash off to school. She was undeviating in her professionalism and devotion to her work.

Mrs. Browning wasn't chummy. She didn't gossip, curry friendships with students or ask personal questions like some teachers do. Consequently, she didn't inspire the affection that

Mrs. Browning, my twelfth-grade English teacher.

the light-hearted, "cool" teachers did. But in retrospect, I appreciate her and know I learned more from her than from any other two or three instructors combined. She didn't nag or call out the slackers in class, but expected everyone to step up and do the work correctly. She gave detailed instructions on how to write a term paper: where to type the footnotes, the bibliography and index. She set a timetable for completing each task. I missed several deadlines—it took me years to develop a fraction of her discipline—but the example she set never left me.

I never got the satisfaction of thanking Mrs. Shafer or Mrs. Browning in their lifetime. But in 2015 when I opened a Facebook page called "You Know You're From West Covina If...," I saw an old photo of my seventh-grade English teacher, Henry

Nyeholt. The memories flooded in and I decided to search for him online.

Mister Rogers' Neighborhood hadn't aired yet, but in seventh grade Mr. Nyeholt was *my* Mister Rogers—someone who makes you feel comfortable and safe. On the surface he couldn't have been more different. Whereas Fred Rogers was plain and dweeby, Mr. Nyeholt was dashing and fit. But in the most important way Mr. Nyeholt was similar: He had a calm, steady voice, never lost his temper and never spoke sharply to anyone. He listened and treated his students with respect. Consequently, no one acted out in class.

When I saw his picture in 2015, I remembered what a great guy he was. I googled his name and amazingly found Mr. Nyeholt right away. He was still living in West Covina fifty-two years later, and his address and phone number were online. I dialed his number.

"I'd like to speak with Henry Nyeholt," I said when a man

answered the phone. It was his son-in-law. He asked why I was calling and when I said I'd been a student of Mr. Nyeholt years ago, he stepped away to bring my teacher to the phone. I was nervous. "Mr. Nyeholt," I said when he picked up. "I'm sure you don't remember me but you were my English teacher at Cameron Junior High."

"Ohh? Well, you must be old!" he joked.

Mr. Nyeholt, my seventh-grade English teacher.

"I am. I found you online and I just want to tell you what fond memories I have of being in your English class. You were kind and you treated your students with respect. You were a wonderful teacher and I want to thank you."

There was a brief pause. "That's very kind of you," he said. I think he was startled, maybe choked up.

Mr. Nyeholt told me he was ninety-one, still married to his wife of sixty-six years, and had retired many years earlier. I felt shy and didn't know what to say next, so I wished him well and said goodbye. The phone call lasted three minutes at most.

The next day I emailed three friends who were at Cameron Junior High with me. When each responded and said how much they liked Mr. Nyeholt (April: "He was kind, soft-spoken"; Donna: "I appreciated him for motivating us to find an interest to study on our own all year"; Alan: "I owe him big time"), I decided to print out their remarks and mail them to our former teacher.

Two weeks later I received a letter from Mr. Nyeholt's daughter, telling me how gratified her dad was to receive the phone call and subsequent testimonials in the mail. I loved that. Three years later, I googled Mr. Nyeholt again and read that he died in December 2017. I learned he was a Navy veteran. A father of five, grandfather of ten. He taught school for thirty-five years. What the obit didn't say was that, like most schoolteachers, he was probably under-celebrated, under-rewarded.

There are bad teachers in everyone's life; I had my share. The great ones are a rare and wonderful occurrence. If you have the opportunity to thank a teacher who's still living, do it now. For yourself, and for that person whose gift will always be with you.

Dan, Mom, I, Dave and Dad waiting for the show to start in a Vegas showroom, 1963.

Chapter Eight
Dad's Las Vegas, My Las Vegas

M y dad loved Las Vegas. The glamour and sass, the bravado. He loved the chiming bustle of the casinos, the celebrity spotting, the chance to briefly feel like a big shot and maybe score a few bucks at the gaming tables.

Dad grew up in Chicago, and he carried with him the raw, uninhibited grit of that city. I think he was out of place in California, even after he'd lived here fifty years. His buddies were Italian American, rough around the edges, and they'd all migrated, like him, from the Midwest or East Coast. You had Cado Cosentino, the grocer who brayed like a donkey and lived beyond his means; Rocco Calarco, the all-seeing barber with the soft voice and Don Ameche moustache; and Vince Manno, who ran a TV repair shop and named his daughters Amelia and Philomena.

Dad's buddies had connections in Vegas, the possible implications of which didn't occur to me for a long time. In the 1960s, the Mafia ran that racy town. Once a year, Dad took our family to Vegas for a weekend vacation but curiously he never booked a hotel in advance. We'd rise at 4 a.m. to avoid driving in the punishing Mojave Desert heat and arrive four hours later at the Riviera or the Sahara, both popular joints on the Strip. Inside the air-conditioned lobby with its shiny mid-century décor, Dad would approach the front desk and drop the name of

Las Vegas Strip in the early 1960s.

somebody who was a very good friend of somebody at the hotel. An assistant manager would glide out from behind a partition, smooth and glossy. "Hello, Marv. Yes, I believe we can accommodate you and your family."

I'm not saying Rocco, Cado, and the rest of Dad's Italian buddies were wise guys, but in my fertile imagination they might've had connections to the lower rungs of that flashy extended family that dominated Vegas. Maybe.

A weekend in Vegas was our family's once-a-year slice of living large. In the daytime Dad shot craps and played poker in the casino. Mom read books poolside and my brothers and I swam in the enormous pool, played "Marco Polo," and squabbled. There was something fun and something charged—literally— about staying in a big modern Vegas hotel. If you scooted your shoes along the hallway carpet and then pressed the elevator button, you'd get a tiny shock.

At night Dad treated us to dinner and a big-ticket nightclub act in one of the showrooms along the Strip. He loved playing big spender and slipping the maître d' a twenty-dollar bill—$200 in today's currency—to secure a good table near the stage. Once settled in a posh banquette he'd sit up straight, shoulders back, and lift his chin to acknowledge the specialness of the occasion. In a formal voice reserved for such moments he'd say, "What do you wish?" to my brothers and me, inviting us to select from a menu of lobster, filet mignon, sweetbreads, and flaming desserts. Wow.

We saw Johnny Carson do his nightclub act one year, Donald O'Connor the next, and in 1966 caught Bobby Darin and an unknown, opening-act comic named Richard Pryor. The Vietnam War was raging and when Pryor did a silly bit about a fumbling Navy man on a submarine, the inebriated mother of a dead serviceman stood up in the audience, shouted "Up yours!" and stormed out. Pryor never recovered his cool. His set was ruined.

In the early '60s, the era of *Ocean's Eleven* and the Rat Pack, Vegas was totally different from today. With 100,000 residents, the Las Vegas metropolitan area had about five percent of today's population, and even with a certain tacky sheen it didn't

The Riviera, my favorite Las Vegas hotel.

approach the aggressively grotesque grandiosity that exists now. The Desert Inn resort had a country-club ambience and its own golf course. The town wasn't overbuilt. Along the Strip between the Sands and the Flamingo, the Stardust and the Tropicana, there were vacant lots with tumbleweed and creosote bush. Instead of nonstop glitz you'd see liquor stores, gas stations, a drive-in movie theater, and several low-priced motels—the Tallyho, the Lotus Inn, the Wagon Wheel—with promises of frosty AC, silver-dollar jackpots, and cheap steak-and-eggs breakfast.

One afternoon Dad took us to the Desert Inn where Phil Harris, fresh off his golf game, was holding court like a bon vivant in the lobby. Nobody knows who Phil Harris was any more, but he was married to the 1940s movie star Alice Faye and did the voice of Baloo the Bear in Disney's *The Jungle Book*. Vegas was much more relaxed in those days, the celebrities less guarded. One year I saw Phyllis Diller enter the back door of the Sahara, looking like a tourist with a cluster of big shopping bags. I was even more entertained when Eddie Gevirtz dove into the pool at the Sahara. Gevirtz was a wacky Los Angeles TV personality who owned Regal Furs and hawked his pelts on the local pro-wrestling telecasts. He was a furrier by trade, which struck my brothers and me as hysterically funny when we saw his extremely hirsute body in swim trunks.

I was extremely starstruck as a kid. One year at the Riviera Peggy Lee was headlining and somehow I discovered her room number. Full of chutzpah, I left a large picture postcard under her door asking for an autograph with a special request that she have it delivered to my room. Today Miss Lee would be ensconced out of town in a gated community, or in a hotel penthouse with a secure private elevator. And here's an interesting footnote: the following year our family stayed again at the Riviera and Liberace was headlining. I remember looking out the window of our hotel room and seeing the name of his opening act on the marquee: an up-and-comer named Barbra Streisand.

That was the summer of 1963. I knew who Streisand was—she'd been on *The Ed Sullivan Show* and her first album was rising on the charts—but I didn't know enough to urge my parents to take us to see her first gig in the western United

Liberace, 1968. *Photo by Jac. de Nijs.*

States. Years later I read that Liberace championed Barbra and insisted she open for him. When the Vegas audience chattered during her set, Liberace decided to walk on stage at the top of each show—no doubt in a sequined tuxedo and voluminous fox-fur coat—and introduce Streisand as his exciting new discovery. With that stamp of approval from the world's highest-paid entertainer, the blue-haired Liberace diehards got quiet and paid respect to the girl with the Modigliani face and thrilling voice.

A few years later, my dad, my brother Dave and I were at LAX. This was before airport security got tight, so we were walking down a long corridor to greet the plane my grandmother was arriving on. Coming toward us in an electric cart we spot the very same Liberace, looking grand and starlike and working the room as if he were a float at the Rose Parade. "Lee baby, how are ya?" my dad called out in a loud voice. Liberace indulged us with an enormous grin and a regal wave. You could take Liberace out of Vegas but you couldn't take Vegas out of Liberace. Or out of my dad.

My Aunt Rollie at the Field Museum in Chicago, 1992.

Chapter Nine

Aunt Rollie Conquers the Universe

My Aunt Rosalyn was tiny, just barely five feet. She was formidable and shrewd. Vain and imperious. Exasperating and inflexible. I loved her.

I loved her because she took time to sit with me when I was growing up and asked me questions in a way no one else asked. She really listened. I loved her because she sent me an annual birthday card with a check for five dollars—long past the point when five dollars meant anything.

I even loved her after she was horrible to my mother and refused, throughout a decade-long estrangement, to consider that her own vanity had fueled a foolish, deluded grudge.

My brothers and I called her Rollie, at her request, and in my first four-and-a-half years, before our family moved from Chicago to California, she was a vivid presence in our lives. I remember thinking very early of my mother, grandmother, and Rollie as a female triumvirate, each one vital and significant in my life. I probably thought everyone had a Rollie.

She was born Rosalyn Lina Guthmann in 1903, the oldest of three children and my father's senior by eleven years. Her father David Raphael Guthmann was a short-tempered man who ran the household like a dictator, keeping my grandma Sadie on a short financial leash. In addition to my dad, Marvin, there was another brother, Dave. Three years Rollie's junior, he was the black sheep, a loner and a misfit. It was Marvin who became her adored favorite: Even when he battled my brothers and me and unleashed his horrible temper, Rollie remained blind to his demons and admonished me during her annual visits to consider each conflict from his point of view.

When she was twenty-five, Rollie married Dick Harris, who was ten years older and so accommodating that, for all I know, they never fought. "He had the most wonderful disposition of anybody I ever met," she enthused many years after his death. "That man never said anything not nice about anybody."

In the 1930s and '40s, the Harrises operated a radio-repair shop in Chicago called Radio Doctors. Soft-spoken Uncle Dick was ostensibly the co-proprietor, but anyone who set foot in the shop knew instantly who ran the show. Rollie kept the books and payroll, stood hawk-eyed behind repairmen while they fixed equipment and decided when, if ever, employees got a raise.

"I was the one who had to fight," she remembered. "Fight

Rosalyn and Dick Harris, Chicago World's Fair, 1933.

with the suppliers, fight with the customers. Dick would just say, 'Wait, I'll call the boss's daughter.' That was me: 'The Daughter.' "

Rollie had two sons, both of whom inherited her bluntness and initiative. She was their disciplinarian: "If the boys were naughty, Dick told me, 'You ought to punish them.' He never did. So I would go in the bathroom and sit on the toilet seat and spank them. Then I'd go in my room and cry."

Bob, her first and favorite, dutifully phoned his mother every day of his life. Donald, her second, shared her lake-view apartment at 6118 North Sheridan Drive throughout his forties and fifties. Most nights he slept at his girlfriend Sarah's place, then came home for breakfast, showered, and changed for work. At day's end he was back at his mother's for dinner. The bond was fierce.

Rosalyn was much, much tougher on women than on men. Her siblings and children were all men, and their wives were subject to her scrutiny. She saw herself as having a man's compe-

Rollie at Radio Doctors, the repair shop she ran with her husband Dick, 1937.

tence, backbone, and self-reliance, and she considered many women weak and untrustworthy. "I'm so glad I was born a woman," she once told me, "so I didn't have to marry one."

Rollie wasn't happy when both her brothers married non-Jewish women, and she predictably took a dim view of Donald's girlfriend. One afternoon, after Donald moved out and bought a house in the suburbs, Sarah served meat loaf, mashed potatoes, and a simple green salad. Rollie was polite during the meal, but when Donald and Sarah went to the kitchen I saw the disapproval on her face. "So what did you think of that?" she asked me. "Oh, it was fine," I said cautiously. One side of her mouth curled in disgust. "I call that shiksa food," she said.

Rollie didn't spare her grandson's first wife, either, especially when they decided to marry right out of high school. "How do you know you want to spend your life with her when she's the only girl you ever dated?" she asked. "You don't go to the library and check out the same book every time, do you? No! You read a lot of books, so you know what you like."

And here's another thing about Rollie: she was frugal to an extreme. "She was so tight with the buck," my dad recalled, "that your Uncle Dick used to steal a couple o' bucks out of the till [at Radio Doctors] when she wasn't looking." She never purchased furniture or housewares but brought things home from the thrift store where she volunteered. Her sofa and chairs were covered in plastic. Even the plastic grapes on the coffee table were dust-guarded by a transparent plastic tea cozy. Rollie never traveled, never dined in expensive restaurants. Most people enjoy spending money, but Rollie's thrill was *not* spending it. It made her feel secure; it made her feel as if she'd won the game.

This was perfectly loony, given that Rollie had tons of money —far more, we later discovered, than anyone suspected. She had it precisely because she never spent it. "You're a wealthy woman," my dad said once. "Why don't you enjoy it?" "I don't know *how*," she answered, a bit pitifully.

During her annual visits to California, when my brothers and I were kids, Rollie initiated a game called "Store." Out came the card table, which represented a retail sales counter. Danny, Davey, and I gathered random items from around the house, arranged them on the table, attached price tags, and awaited our first customer.

The door opened and Mrs. Harris entered with great dignity —posture erect, carrying a purse full of Monopoly money. "Hello, young man," she said with great formality. "May I see your merchandise?" This was our cue to describe the items on the table and state their price. Bartering might ensue, then an exchange of money. Here we learned to carefully make change. Once satisfied, our consumer brought her commerce to a close. Purse snapped shut, she bid us a gracious good day and regally exited the room.

In Rollie's realm, thrift, caution and prudent budgeting were everything. "You don't pay any attention to finance, Eddie," she said gravely when I was in my forties. "You *should*. Finance is very important—it has to do with almost everything. The reason Hitler got so strong is he was a sharp guy and he figured, 'The Jews have the money and I'm going to get their money.' Why do you think he wanted to kill all those Jews? He was envious. He wanted what they had and baby, he got it."

Rollie and I were a mutual affection society. I had a soft spot for her, because she was so unlike anyone I'd ever known, because she was good to me, and because she said exactly what she thought—whether or not you cared to hear it. As an adult I visited her periodically, and in 1987 I interviewed her on videotape talking about her early life. She spoke with warm affection of her four grandparents, each of whom lived in Chicago when she was young, cried when remembering my dad as a baby ("so cute"), and cried again when she described my grandmother, so undervalued by my grandfather, as "a lady."

On another visit I videotaped Rollie at the Michael Reese Service League Thrift Shop, where she volunteered every Satur-

Rollie and I in her apartment at 6118 North Sheridan Road, 1992.

Rollie with her brothers, my dad Marvin and my Uncle Dave. At my brother Dave's wedding in Seattle, 1987.

day for almost forty years. On camera I caught her busting the store manager's cajones and—without missing a beat—turning around and sweet-talking her favorite customer into another purchase. "She buys a lot of stuff," Rollie said to the camera with a wide-eyed stage whisper.

Later the same year, Rollie flew to Seattle for my brother Dave's wedding, where the incident occurred that frosted her against my mother. As the wedding was about to begin, my parents were seated in the front pew with Mom's sisters, Esther and Winifred. Seeing that Uncle Dave was in the second row with his daughters and grandchildren, Mom suggested Rollie sit with them. Seemed logical, since she was staying with Dave's daughter Lynn. Rollie complied but it later came out that she considered this an outrageous affrontery and seethed with resentment. As the self-defined matriarch, she expected the ultimate deference. She thought she should be in the front row.

When they saw each other again in Chicago, after several years' absence, Mom smiled and approached Rollie for a hug. Rollie stiffened her shoulders and took a dramatic step backwards. "I see you have a very short memory," she sniffed, head held high. Her rebuke chilled the air. Mom sat on the sofa, trembling, and Donald's girlfriend held her hand. No one said, "Rosalyn, you're out of line. Apologize to Roberta." Not my dad. Not either of Rollie's adult sons. Amazing how much power that woman wielded.

My dad spent years trying to reason her out of her grudge, and when Rollie complained to me about the perceived slight I reminded her that my mother visited Grandma Guthmann every day in the nursing home where she died. (Rosalyn was home in Chicago, having ceded the care of her mother to my dad and mom.) "My mother saw Grandma every day and treated her as if she were her own mother," I argued. "Can't you let *that* guide your opinion of her?" It was useless: there was no dissuading Rollie from a fixed position, especially as she grew more rigid with age.

My mother, the least spiteful person I've ever known, weathered the rift with dignity and not a little puzzlement. She even made a point of saying to me, "I don't want you to feel that you need to cut yourself off from Rosalyn because of this situation." Classy lady.

Finally, after 10 years, a détente occurred when Rollie's memory faltered and she forgot what she was angry about. A civil encounter followed, brokered by my dad. When I spoke to Rollie on the phone later she asked, in all sincerity, "Why did you never explain to me what really happened at Davey's wedding? No one ever told me!"

I didn't see Rollie the last five years of her life. I was told she was frail and depressed, and when I called my cousin Bobby he discouraged my visiting ("It wouldn't be very rewarding"). She had a series of live-in caretakers, but her complaints were so relentless that, one by one, the caretakers all quit. Eventually, the agency refused to send anyone new.

Rollie died in 1999, at ninety-six, having experienced nearly the entire twentieth century. Two months later I received a letter from my cousin Donald in the mail. I knew it was an inheritance check—Rollie always promised me I'd be remembered in her will—but when I opened the envelope I saw that my bequest was only $10,000. I'm embarrassed to say I expected a lot more, even hoped it would expedite my retirement. Eventually I saw it as a life lesson: Never adjust your future plans in expectation of a financial gift.

When Rollie died, everyone was astonished at the size of her estate. We always knew she'd assiduously hoarded her money. But $30 million? That's $56 million in 2025 currency. Seventy percent of it went to the IRS because she didn't shelter it properly, and the rest to her sons, her two grandchildren, and the Lincoln Park Zoo in Chicago. Posthumously, the zoo honored her generosity by naming a baby gorilla "Rollie."

Chapter Ten
The Year I Played in *Oliver!*

Starting at age seven or eight, I dreamed of being an actor. I remember running through an open field near my house, pretending I was dodging enemy fire in an action movie called *Rifles of Revenge*. I fantasized the plaudits I'd earn as a child star. Fame, adulation, an Academy Award. I could taste them all.

None of this came to pass, but when I was fifteen my chutzpah landed me a debut on the professional stage. The Carousel Theatre, a newly opened theater-in-the-round in West Covina, was staging a season of Broadway revivals. *Oliver!* was on the schedule and Georgia Brown, star of the original London and Broadway productions, would repeat her role as Nancy, the tragic slattern who rescues Oliver Twist.

With beginner's naiveté, I wrote a letter to Danny Dare, one of the Carousel's two producers and co-owners: "Dear Mr. Dare, I live in West Covina and I'm a talented actor. I can do an excellent English accent and I can sing. You should cast me in *Oliver!*" I didn't tell him I had no formal training in acting, singing, or dancing and no stage experience apart from school assemblies and high-school drama class.

Amazingly, Mr. Dare phoned and invited me to his office at the Carousel. I think he was amused. I'm sure my mother drove me—West Covina had no bus service—and dropped me off with a dime and instructions to call when my big meeting was over. I stepped into Mr. Dare's office, and although I don't remember what he asked or what I said to sell myself, the conversation ended with him saying, "Well, let's go inside the theater and see how you move onstage."

Moments later, Mr. Dare introduced me to the director David Tihmar and instructed him to incorporate me into one of the crowd scenes—maybe the one where the villain Bill Sikes clubs Nancy to death on London Bridge as she's delivering Oliver Twist to his freedom. I guess something went right, because the next thing I knew I was in wardrobe being fitted as a working-class Londoner of the Edwardian era.

At fifteen, I was too old and too tall to play one of Fagin's orphans, so there went my chance to sing "Food, Glorious Food" and lark about with a fake, guttersnipe Cockney accent. Instead, I became a member of the chorus. I was in "Oom-Pah-Pah," the upbeat musical number in a tavern that opens Act Two, and I was a generic upper-class Londoner in "Who Will Buy?"

For "Consider Yourself," I had to learn some simple dance steps called a cakewalk—but with no experience and no assistance I was lost. Zoya Leporska, a bottle-blond Russian choreographer, made exactly one appearance during our week of rehearsals. Since several cast members had played *Oliver!* at the Melodyland The-

atre in Anaheim the previous season, she ran them through the cakewalk quickly and didn't bother to take me aside and show me the steps. Poof! She was gone.

The Carousel Theater in West Covina.

So I learned by doing. I cringe remembering the mistakes I made in "Consider Yourself" during rehearsal. Looking back I wonder why they kept me in the show, but I guess I was cute and enthusiastic. Mr. Tihmar must've thought I was OK, or maybe Moose Peting, the amiable assistant director, put in a good word for me.

Moose, who contrary to his name was small in stature, was one of several colorful characters in our company. Alan "Boomie" DeWitt, the first flamboyant queen I'd ever met, would sashay backstage cooing "Moose, darling!" to his best buddy. Boomie was very tall and wore glasses, and according to Moose he once decked a stagehand who mocked his fluttery hands and mincing walk. If you look closely at *A Star Is Born* with Judy Garland, Boomie plays one of the makeup artists who inflict an ugly makeover on Judy's Esther Blodgett character. Excuse my brag, but that makes me just two degrees separated from Judy Garland, theatrically speaking.

Mr. Tihmar was also gay, but of a different variety than Boomie. He dressed impeccably, exuded an aristocratic air, and having been a hoofer on Broadway in *Oklahoma!* he moved

The wonderful Yiddish actor Leo Fuchs. He played Fagin.

with a dancer's grace. "I don't mind amateurism, in its place," he said grandly at rehearsal one day. "What I *can't* bear is unprofessionalism." He wasn't a bit out—few gay men were at that time—but one of my fellow chorus members swore he padded his crotch with "plastic fruit" to simulate a large basket. I'm still not sure what "plastic fruit" entails.

Victor Stiles, who acted in the movie *Santa Claus Conquers the Martians* with Pia Zadora, had the title role of Oliver Twist. He was fourteen and his voice had dropped, so it was agonizing to hear him assault the tender high notes on "Where Is Love?" Leo Fuchs, a Yiddish theater veteran and total mensch, played Fagin, foxy den father to a tribe of pickpockets. Mr. Fuchs (pronounced "Fyooks") was beloved by all and an absolute contrast to Georgia Brown, an icy diva who thought this down-market gig was beneath her. I get that: Lionel Bart, composer of the

Oliver! score, wrote the part of Nancy expressly for Georgia, and our suburban theater-in-the round probably felt like chintzy chicken feed after Broadway and London's West End.

Oliver! was also my introduction to the catty, envy-fueled gossip that thrives in the dressing rooms of lesser players and chorus members. A lot of the buzz centered on male celebrities who were secretly "queer." Rock Hudson was mentioned and that turned out to be true, but some of the guys claimed Kirk Douglas, Burt Lancaster, and Elvis Presley were also members of the lavender league. That sounded like hooey to me, even at fifteen.

I loved my time with *Oliver!* I adored being part of a company and hearing their gypsy tales of theaters they'd played and legends they'd performed with. I loved leaving my name each night on the sign-in sheet posted inside the stage door—a theatrical tradition that lets the stage manager know you're in the house. The blank boxes on the sign-up sheet were tiny, so everyone signed their initials only. I concocted a continuous cursive squiggle that connected the end of my capital E with the start of my capital G. I still use that squiggle today.

I loved hearing Georgia Brown's gutsy delivery of "As Long As He Needs Me" each night, and to this day I remember the lyrics to most of the songs in *Oliver!* I felt a special thrill when friends came to see the

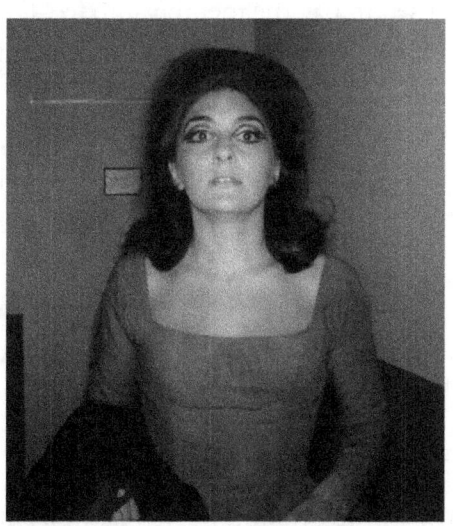

Georgia Brown: A great voice and a diva's frosty hauteur.

show; when I recognized teachers and the West Covina High School librarian in the audience; when my mother attended a matinee with her friend Edwina "Eddie" Tisch, who dressed in black.

Oliver! closed its two-week run in July 1966, and I slipped into quiet, downcast withdrawal. Now that I had my foot in the show business door, I wanted more. A production of Peter Weiss's intense drama *Marat/Sade* was set to open at the Carousel in a couple of months, and when I asked Moose Peting how I might get cast, he smiled indulgently and said there wasn't a chance in hell. *Marat/Sade* was a touring company and was cast in London and New York with seasoned actors. Oh, hell.

Oliver! was a feather in my cap, and now that I'd scored my first professional stage credit I was eligible to join Actors' Equity, the union for performers in live theater. I was fired up with the desire to be a professional actor. I don't remember what it cost to join Equity, but I remember sobbing when my parents refused to pay the membership fee. I'd been so lucky to get cast in *Oliver!*—a fluke, really—and now my dream of being in showbiz was derailed. Maybe this was my parents' way of sparing me the torments of a cutthroat business.

Still, I hungered for another break. I wrote to the producers of *A Separate Peace* and *Mr. and Mrs. Bo Jo Jones*, two movies in development with adolescent characters, but since I lacked an agent or the tiniest connection, I didn't hear back. I acted in high school and college theater and won an honorable mention at a regional drama competition playing Jonathan Rosepettle in *Oh Dad, Poor Dad, Mamma's Hung You in the Closet and I'm Feeling So Sad*. But I wasn't all that great and I never got the proper training. I had natural comic timing, and I was good with accents and dialogue, but physically I was clenched and self-conscious. That's death for an actor.

And yet there remained a strong need on my part to act. To be accepted and seen, to disappear inside a character and kick out the jams. Paul Newman described the urge perfectly: "Acting gave me a sanctuary where I was able to create emotions without being penalized for having them."

Moving to San Francisco after college, I still wanted to act. But auditions were traumatic, and aside from parts in two tiny independent movies, both directed by friends, and a few months with a children's theater troupe that played shopping malls and county fairs, I didn't book any gigs.

Instead of a life on the boards, I gravitated to journalism and became an arts reporter and movie critic at the *San Francisco Chronicle*. I'm not sorry I didn't pursue acting more diligently. I can't afford those regrets, and I doubt I would have survived the disappointments and rejection. I still sometimes imagine being a professional actor—speaking Spanish in a Pedro Almodóvar film is a favorite fantasy—but I'm happy to observe the experts doing the work.

Chapter Eleven

Reefer Madness: An Encounter with Anti-Weed Hysteria

Martha Lupton Schneidewind was the name of my high school journalism teacher. A tall, birdlike woman, she wore wool suits and ladylike scarves and had a quick, scampering walk. She was kind, loquacious, and, to my insensitive teenage self, amusingly absurd with her chirping voice and outdated phraseology.

During the mid-1960s teenage drug abuse was a huge bugaboo in suburbs like West Covina. One day Mrs. Schneidewind entered the journalism lab and announced that local policemen had just spoken to the high school faculty about marijuana—a presentation that included the lighting of a joint. If teachers could detect the whiff of weed, the reasoning went, the school could more readily deliver student miscreants to the cops and boost the city's anti-pot crusade.

"It's unusually fragrant," Mrs. S. remarked without a trace of irony when a student asked how the reefer smelled. "Not at all unpleasant."

Within a few days I was assigned to write an editorial about marijuana for our campus paper, the *Spartan Shield*. Mrs. Schneidewind didn't indicate an angle or point of view the editorial should follow, so I figured I had free rein.

I hadn't smoked weed yet (that would happen the spring of

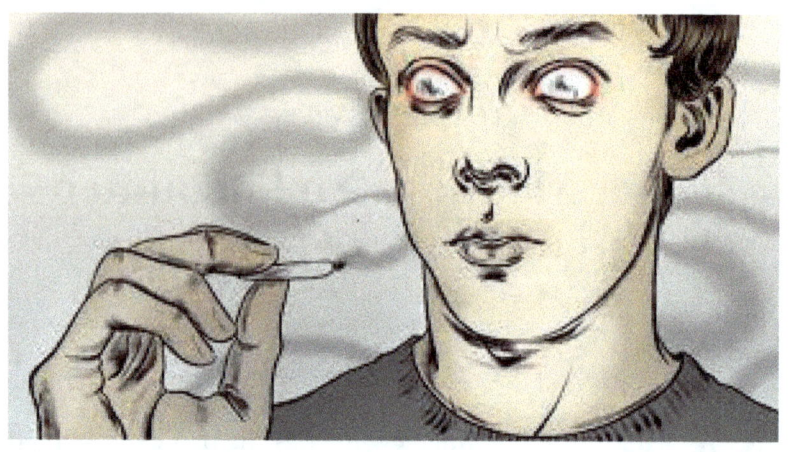

my senior year), but my brother Dan had already been busted for possession, and, like most teenagers, I was intrigued by anything that could make masses of grown-ups so freaking scared. There was an immature, forbidden glamour that accrued to drug culture in those days, an excitement that even cannabis virgins like myself could appreciate from listening to the Beatles' "Sgt. Pepper's Lonely Hearts Club Band" or Grace Slick's piercing vocal on the song "White Rabbit" ("Ree-ee-member! What the dormouse said! 'Feed your head! Feed your he-he-he-head!!' "

To write the editorial, I referenced a booklet I'd bought at the Free Press Bookstore, a hipster haven in the Fairfax District of Los Angeles. The booklet had a glossary of terms about marijuana ("bomber" was a big fat joint, "pinner" a thin joint), and I naively incorporated those terms into my piece to simulate a streetwise, insider's perspective.

It didn't occur to me at the time, and I have no proof, but I suspect my marijuana assignment originated with the West Covina Police Department. I say this because when I finished the editorial and submitted it to Mrs. Schneidewind, she sent it to the assistant principal Barbara Buch for approval. Miss Buch, I now believe, was deputized by the West Covina PD to contrive the *Spartan Shield* editorial.

Miss Buch (rhymes with "spook") was an odd lady. Although it was her job to enforce the dress code for girls—skirts could be no more than an inch above the knee—her own sartorial style would have to be described as Aging Stripper. She wore a cake of makeup, shaped her eyebrows like arched caterpillars, and favored sexy blouses and wide patent-leather belts that emphasized her generous bosom. According to a persistent campus rumor—total myth, easily dispelled—Miss Buch was a former *Playboy* centerfold.

I never spoke with Miss Buch, but a day or two after submitting my marijuana editorial I was taken aside by Mrs. Schneidewind. From her desk drawer, she extracted my typewritten copy and showed me the additions Miss Buch had made to my editorial—additions that totally altered what I'd written.

Among her gems was this ridiculous sentence: "The casual marijuana user may embark on his drug experiment innocently enough, only to emerge from his 'high' with needle marks on his arm."

I'd never tried recreational drugs of any kind, but I could recognize anti-drug hysteria. "That sentence needs to come out," I protested. "I didn't write that and it's not true."

"I'm sorry," Mrs. Schneidewind replied. "But this is final, Ed. The editorial will run this way." Worse yet, it ran that way with my byline.

Vintage anti-marijuana propaganda.

Looking back, I imagine Mrs. Schneidewind felt trapped—that if she resisted Miss Buch's edict and defended my journalistic honor she'd be risking her job. I never knew her to be unethical or heavy-handed on other occasions—in fact, we remained friends and stayed in touch until she died in 2000—so I feel certain that was the case. But my sense of betrayal at the time was deep and painful.

A few months later, I smoked my first joint with Flip Farrall, another member of the *Spartan Shield* staff. Most weed came from Mexico back then, and when you bought an ounce ("a lid") it was mostly seeds and stems. Terribly weak. I remember taking long drags, trying to inhale properly and get a buzz. It took a while to get the hang of it. And no, fergawdsakes, I never woke up with effing needle marks in my arms.

Today, I still occasionally get high and sometimes use cannabinoid-based edibles for sleep and pain. I feel grateful that marijuana prohibition finally came to an end in California in 2016. I wish Fraulein Buch had lived to see the day.

Chapter Twelve

Bobby Kennedy and the
Year That Took Him

When you're seventeen and the world is shifting around you, when your hero is killed and the air seems charged with an ionic force that was never there before, it takes a long time to figure out what it means and how you've been changed by it all.

That's what 1968 was like for me. Martin Luther King Jr. and Robert F. Kennedy were killed that year. In August, Chicago Mayor Richard Daley sanctioned police riots at the Democratic National Convention. In November the unimaginable occurred when Richard Nixon, who'd lost in his 1960 presidential bid, and was widely reviled and thought to be politically dead, was elected president.

I graduated from high school that year, and in the weeks leading up to the June 4th California primary I was an eager, idealistic volunteer in Robert Kennedy's campaign to become the Democratic Party nominee for president. My friend Geri Soto and I spent countless hours canvassing precincts, peddling Kennedy buttons and bumper stickers, stapling posters to utility poles and replacing them when Eugene McCarthy volunteers tore them down.

One night during a fundraising rally at the Los Angeles Sports Arena, I briefly left the auditorium to find the men's

On the campaign trail.

room. I was surprised to see Bobby standing alone in the corner of a wide corridor, apparently concentrating on the speech he was about to give. I hesitated—could that really be him?—and then approached him and shook his hand. Within seconds a dozen or more thrilled Kennedy supporters surrounded him until a pair of security guards rushed to his side and whisked him away. There was a fervor and idolatry in Bobby's fans. They responded to him in the same way fans respond to Taylor Swift today, or the way they responded to Frank Sinatra in the 1940s.

A lot of people didn't like Bobby. Among a certain liberal elite, it was fashionable to scorn him as a ruthless opportunist and exploiter of his brother John Kennedy's legacy. After all,

Bobby didn't announce his candidacy until March 16, several months after Eugene McCarthy entered the race and demonstrated that a peace candidate could successfully challenge the unpopular incumbent President Lyndon Johnson.

People were suspicious of a man who'd made the mistake of working for the red-baiting Senator Joseph R. McCarthy back in 1953. They cried nepotism when Bobby was appointed attorney general by JFK and resented his election as U.S. senator from New York when his original home state was Massachusetts. What many didn't grasp was how much he'd changed during his years of public service.

In his book *Robert Kennedy: A Memoir*, Jack Newfield described "the shock of unrecognition" that people often felt when they met him—the feeling that Bobby's gentle demeanor was at odds with his reputation for ruthlessness. In *Harper's Magazine*, David Halberstam wrote, "Most politicians seem attractive from a distance but under closer examination they fade; the vanities, the pettiness, the vulgarities come out. Robert Kennedy was different. Under closer inspection he was far more winning than most."

Bobby had the gift of empathy, the ability to see the world through the eyes of the poor, the unrepresented, the victims of racial and social prejudice. That's a rare commodity in a politician and one that can't be faked. Whereas his opponent Eugene McCarthy was brilliant, professorial and cold in manner, Bobby brought warmth, spontaneity, and the charisma of a rock star.

During the last week of Bobby's California primary campaign, Geri and I drove to Los Angeles for a series of rallies at Kennedy campaign headquarters at the Ambassador Hotel. On Sunday night, June 2, we stood in the Embassy Ballroom of the hotel, surrounded by a sea of red, white, and blue boaters, and

Bobby with civil right activist Cesar Chavez.

cheered when he quoted George Bernard Shaw: "Some men see things as they are and ask, 'Why?' I dream things that never were and ask, 'Why not?'"

I was stunned by the wild enthusiasm of Bobby's supporters and thrilled by the possibility of a victory in November. To watch him hold an audience was amazing. Bobby had a playful side. I remember him saying he couldn't trust Californians to get out and vote. "After all, you're the ones who elected Ronald Reagan governor," he teased in a singsong-y voice: "*Oh no we didn't!*" came back the collective reply. "Oh yes, you *did*," he chided.

It chills me to write this, but I also remember thinking how vulnerable he looked in that ballroom—how easy it might be for some lunatic to take a shot. Throughout the campaign, Geri and I frequently heard the refrain, "Why waste your time? He's gonna get killed just like his brother." Those words felt cruel, but when they became true no one was altogether surprised.

Two nights later, in the early morning hours of June 5, Bobby gave his victory speech at the Ambassador Hotel and was gunned down moments later. I was at home and had gone to sleep, confident of a Kennedy victory, before the late election returns. I didn't hear the news until the following morning, when my mother told me at breakfast that Bobby Kennedy was lying in a coma. Roughly eighteen hours later, he was gone. He was forty-two.

There was one week of school left, and I walked through final exams, commencement exercise and graduation with numbness, confusion, and unarticulated grief. At seventeen, you don't know how to mourn. I joined the Kennedy Action Corps that summer, a coalition of former RFK campaign workers, and canvassed my neighborhood collecting signatures on gun-control petitions. The assassination continued to haunt me. For months afterward, I fantasized how I might have personally prevented Bobby's death by rushing forward to block Sirhan Sirhan's bullets, had I been in the Ambassador Hotel kitchen that night.

After Bobby died, I lost a lot of the trust I once had. I never grew sour on electoral politics, despite that loss; never stopped supporting progressive candidates, social-justice and environmental causes; never lost the conviction that each American deserves a stake in their country.

In my college dorm room, with a Robert F. Kennedy poster by Norman Rockwell.

Chapter Thirteen

Breaking the Redwood Curtain

To my rebellious teenage soul, the University of California at Berkeley sounded like heaven. It was 1968, I was about to graduate from high school and when I pondered college I couldn't imagine a more comfortable fit than the polestar of the student antiwar movement.

Things didn't work out that way. My father hated the idea of my attending a hotbed of radicalism, and since I lacked a scholarship or alternate income source I had to come up with another plan. I pulled out a map of California, studied the location of every state university and chose the campus farthest from home. Humboldt State was 700 miles north—equivalent to the distance between Charleston, South Carolina and Philadelphia, PA.

That's why I chose it: I wanted something dramatically different and far away. Humboldt State, I learned, was located "behind the Redwood Curtain" in Arcata—a sleepy, fogbound town of 8,000 people. Seemingly locked in a political and societal time warp, Humboldt County had two TV channels and two radio stations. The logging industry still thrived, a redneck element actively resented the campus community, and the only restaurant near campus was a greasy spoon with prickly waitresses and the world's worst coffee.

FINAL **DAILY NEWS** **10¢**
NEW YORK'S PICTURE NEWSPAPER

Vol. 51. No. 266 · New York, N.Y. 10011, Friday, May 1, 1970 · WEATHER: Partly cloudy, warm, humid.

NIXON SENDS GIs INTO CAMBODIA

Washington, April 30 (News Bureau)—Several thousand American troops crossed the Vietnam-Cambodian border on orders from President Nixon tonight to attack the Communist main headquarters.

20 miles inside Cambodia. The U.S. force is expected to stay in Cambodia for six to eight weeks. "This is not an invasion of Cambodia," Nixon declared in a nationally televised address from the White House. Earlier story on page 2.

On Guard in Ohio. Unflinching, militant demonstrators on campus of Ohio State University in Columbus stand their ground as national guardsmen hold fixed bayonets to their throats. A total of 1,200 troops and police clashed with students before tear gas dispelled them. Scores were arrested and dozens were injured. —Story p. 3; other pics, centerfold

I'd been on campus a week when I attended my first demonstration. Ronald Reagan, then governor, was meeting with local Republicans at the Carson Mansion, an elaborate Victorian in nearby Eureka. There were twenty or thirty of us on the picket line, shouting slogans and holding placards. We had plenty of reasons to be angry: Reagan had slashed education and mental health spending, authorized police brutality against campus protesters, and alienated environmentalists with his classic remark, "If you've seen one redwood tree, you've seen 'em all."

Reagan was slick, and underneath his affable veneer was a politician who made callous, hard-nosed decisions. I remember him pausing to wave at us malcontents as he entered the mansion—very little security detail that day—and flashing that fixed Hollywood smile as we chanted our disapproval.

Naively, I went back to my dorm room and wrote my parents a detailed letter describing the protest and the antiestablishment sentiments expressed. What was I thinking? Just plain dumb, or maybe I was hoping to tweak my dad's ire. Predictably, the letter I got in return—"I am very perturbed," he wrote—made it clear that my college allowance would expire should I continue to disport myself so recklessly.

Opportunities for dissent didn't abound at Humboldt State. The political fervor in San Francisco, Berkeley, and Oakland was 300 miles away, and in Arcata it was easy to feel cut off from the world. Over the next couple of years, that sense of remoteness and head-in-the-sand disengagement would rapidly change.

My college years, 1968 to 1972, were a time of historic tumult and division in America—but also a time when we felt the imminent rush of profound, widespread change. Nixon kept escalating a corrupt war. In November 1969 we learned that U.S. troops had massacred 500 Vietnamese civilians in the village of My Lai. In May 1970 Nixon bombed Cambodia, and college campuses erupted in indignation. When four unarmed students were killed by the Ohio National Guard at Kent State University, students at hundreds of campuses nationwide went on strike.

Humboldt State was one of them. The day of the Kent State shootings, a spontaneous forum was held on campus in the Sequoia Theater, where people shouted their rage and frustration and struggled to formulate a cogent response. "What can we do?"

The next day a much larger rally took place on the quad between the music, art, and theater buildings. The sun was shining, the air clear and fresh. "There were three to four thousand people there, standing on rooftops," my friend Wesley Chesbro, who later became a California state senator, remembers. "You could hardly squeeze into the plaza." Speeches were made, draft cards were burned, a magnificent singer named Becky Evans brought out her guitar and lifted everyone's hearts. People remained for hours, focused and intent. Anyone who wanted to speak was given a chance. At the end of the rally a vote was taken: The vote by hand for a campus-wide strike was near-unanimous.

It was an unforgettable day, unlike anything previously seen at HSU. Prior to that, the only campus activists were a tiny cadre of shaggy, gloomy Marxists who attracted little support. But on that afternoon in 1970 I remember a collective exhilaration—an awakening. The emotions and commitment generated at that rally forever altered the spirit and culture of Humboldt State and the town of Arcata.

Northtown Bookstore, two blocks off campus, became strike headquarters. Hundreds of people committed to walking precincts to persuade local residents to oppose the war. A lot of them were longhairs who got their first haircut in years in order to interact with the community. One of the strike honchos, Lanny Swerdlow, asked me to organize a teach-in at the local Presbyterian Church. I'd never done anything like that before —I was nineteen—but I booked the speakers, moderated the

Thousands gather on campus to protest the escalating Vietnam War. We voted to strike.

Peace Days festivities followed the campus strike at Humboldt State. I'm in lower part of the frame looking to the left.

event and was amazed when local residents showed up to ask questions or voice opposition to our movement.

Cornelius Siemens, the college president, did a crafty thing by endorsing the strike, thereby deflecting any anger that might misdirect toward the HSU administration. He even joined a small coalition that flew to Washington, D.C., to lobby our state legislators to end the war in Vietnam.

Dr. Siemens was less thrilled with the "memorial bomb crater" that Vietnam Veterans Against the War created just outside the administration building. The vets dug an enormous hole and erected a sign explaining that their purpose wasn't to destroy university property but to make a statement. They carefully separated the topsoil from the subsoil, so the lawn could

Arcata Plaza, the town's commercial hub.

be properly restored when the strike was over—an effort foiled when a bunch of pro-war jocks refilled the crater, shoveling the topsoil in first and the subsoil above it.

The war raged on for another four years and Nixon was inexplicably reelected in 1972, but Humboldt State had effectively rubbed the sleep out of its eyes. The campus, once obscure—once known chiefly for its forestry, wildlife, and oceanography departments—became a haven for lefties, artists, potheads, and spiritual seekers. Admission applications soared. Arcata had a new civic pride and cultural birth with restaurants, a natural foods store and nightclub, two repertory cinemas, and a city council dominated by progressives rather than the pro-timber, anti-hippie old guard.

Although I felt transported to an earlier decade when I first arrived in Arcata, like a character in *The Twilight Zone*, I realized how lucky I was to witness such dynamic change in so short a window of time. Instead of the hard-edged confrontations at Berkeley, where Governor Reagan called in the National Guard and declared martial law—one bystander was killed, another blinded, another shot point-blank in the stomach—Humboldt State developed a gentler, more balanced activism that emphasized community dialogue over rancor.

During the campus strike and the months that followed, Arcata remained a tranquil, easy place to live. Almost no crime. People left their bicycles unlocked, also their front doors. After the strike you could feel a thrum of communal warmth throughout the community. To a great extent, the remoteness of Arcata enhanced that genial small-town vibe. Without the distracting hamster wheel of urban life, one's social options mostly involved the company of good friends. Potluck dinners, walks in the redwoods, bonfires on a rugged Humboldt County beach.

I feel a wave of nostalgia when I remember walking into a friend's house on a Saturday night and hearing Jethro Tull, or the Beatles' *White Album*, or Crosby, Stills & Nash's *Déjà Vu* on the stereo. The murmur of voices, eruptions of laughter. Cheap wine and rose hips tea are served, a joint or two circulate. People sit on beat-up sofas and chairs, on the floor. Friends bring veggie casseroles, zucchini bread and pumpkin bread. Pies made from wild Himalayan berries harvested from a fence outside an abandoned farmhouse. On the stovetop a large pot of lentils simmers, its moisture fogging up the windows against the cool, thick fog that blankets Arcata most nights.

Easy and peaceful. It would be lovely to travel back and merge once more, briefly, with that rich and tangy experience.

Chapter Fourteen

The Unforgettable Mamie Jackson

People remember the summer of 1969 for its historical milestones—the Moon Landing and Woodstock, the Manson murders and Stonewall—but for me there's another landmark event. That was the summer I met the extraordinary Mamie Jackson.

Picture this: I'm living with my parents in West Covina following my freshman year of college. Miserable from the heat and smog, missing my college buddies, chafing at the blandness of suburban Los Angeles.

No job skills, no car. I land a crappy job selling *Life* magazine subscriptions by phone. The office is on the second floor of a seedy strip mall in La Puente, the sales staff a crew of underpaid misfits. The person I immediately notice is the loquacious, larger-than-life Mame Jackson. African American, a native of Hilo, Hawaii, she is twenty-six years old (seems older) and wickedly funny. A substitute teacher with the West Covina Unified School District, Mame works this two-bit gig to pay her rent between terms.

She's a double amputee, the result of surviving a fire at six months old, then spending years in hospitals before losing her legs at age six. One leg is severed above the knee (she calls it "A.K."), and the other below the knee ("B.K."). Her disability

Las Vegas, 1985. Celebrating with Mamie.

is extreme, but Mame is fierce and proud and not to be messed with. She has prosthetic legs that strap on to her stumps and she walks, without crutches, by shifting her hips and shoulders and taking wide, deliberate steps. To mount stairs, she ascends backwards, taking each step slowly and expertly.

Mame and I become fast friends. She has a disinhibition, a flair for shock value and linguistic ornamentation that I've never encountered. She looks a tad like Aretha Franklin and wears muumuus and cardigans and a short brown wig that's often askew. Her voice is loud and carries across crowded rooms. There's an aura of fun, rascality and fearlessness about her. My eighteen-year-old self is fascinated.

"Mister Edwards," she says one Monday, using the nom-de-phone I've adopted since my surname is so difficult, "I went to a muvvah-lous party the other evening. Such beautiful people in attendance." She pauses and grins slightly to acknowledge the campy pretense of her tale. "As is customary at such gatherings the various participants began to polarize into separate conversational clusters. The particular coterie to which I happened to gravitate ... [another pause for dramatic effect] were the intellectuals. And we began to discuss my favorite topic of conversation: theatricality. You know, dramaturgy."

This anecdote is delivered over lunch break, as a sad-looking passel of co-workers sit in a circle eating brown-bag lunches. They don't get Mame at all, and I wonder if a few of them don't suspect she's mocking them by talking over their heads. I know they resent her outstanding sales record. We are telephone solicitors, each assigned a narrow carrel with a rotary-dial phone, stacks of names to call, and a scripted sales pitch. Mame, a gifted wordsmith, loves to improvise and embellish on the spiel.

"Good afternoon, Madame," she will begin, a Hawaiian lilt in her voice, crossed with a thespian's plummy panache. "This is Miss Jackson from the Lincoln Training Center for the Mentally Retarded and Handicapped. We are raising much-needed funds for our school by selling subscriptions to *Life* magazine —a magnanimous portion of which sustains our center and benefits the needy and disadvantaged."

Or something like that. In retrospect, I wonder if the Lincoln Training Center even existed—but that's another story. One day, a woman on the phone cuts Mame off mid-spiel. "Hey lady," she snaps, "what makes you think you are so *damn smart* with your ten-dollar words? I know you're reading from a script." Aghast, Mame affects her haughtiest dowager-empress voice to disabuse the fool of her ignorance:

"Madame, these are *my* words," she announces. "*I... am an English major!*"

Mame sells twice as many subscriptions as anyone else and frequently gloats from across the room. "Oh Mister Edwards!"

she trills merrily. "I just sold another order!" I don't mind her braggadocio. To me, Mame Jackson is hugely entertaining and a respite from the tedium of telephone sales.

I can't recall the other telemarketers, except a rawboned Austrian refugee named Roland (Mame pronounces it "Row-LAWNED"), who invites us for drinks one night at his grubby trailer park, as well as an oversexed pepper-pot whom Mame detests ("I wish the man with the largest penis in the world would insert it in her vagina, and then maybe she'd shut up").

Mame has no love for the office managers, either: the crusty Lillian Cort ("an old lady like Cort needs a good rappin' up the ass once in a while") and the saccharine Miss Hornby, who has the temerity to request cash contributions toward a coworker's baby-shower gift. "Cecilia Hornby has imposed a lot of unprofessionalism on me," Mame sniffs.

Mame's language ranges from bawdy to filthy to ornately elegant. Words have a cascading musical quality coming from her. A boring lecture doesn't make her lose interest but rather "assassinates my enthusiasm." A stylish carpet isn't merely attractive; it's "intrepid." She loves dropping words like sesquipedalian (long-winded), otiose (serving no practical purpose) and consanguinity (related by blood). And instead of saying she's full after a heavy meal, Mame declares, "I've been gourmandizing myself for the last hour; I am completely saturated."

One weekend we meet for lunch at a drab diner on Hacienda Boulevard and I invite my very short, redheaded friend Steve and his twelve-year-old brother Richard. Together with Mame, we form such an odd quartet that we elicit a bewildered scowl from the waitress. Mame clocks the sour baggage up and down, orders steak and eggs and inquires, "Comprenez-vous?" with haughty condescension. When the waitress walks away Mame lifts her nose and proclaims, "I can tell she's very illiterate."

One day I swing by Mame's apartment and she doesn't answer the door. I hear the shower running and when I peek through a parted curtain I see a pair of prosthetic legs on the floor—but no Mame. She has a sense of humor about her legs: When I compliment her on her dress she asks me insinuatingly, "Ohh? And do you like my shoes?" "Well, sure," I respond. "Oh really? And do you like my *legs*?"

Mame loves to catch you off guard. Her humor, raunchy and reckless, is her art form, her means of coping with a lonely, marginalized life. Being disabled and Black makes her a double outsider and being an outsider she can afford to eschew the courtesies that constrain the rest of us. "I'm one hell of a bullshitter," she likes to say. "I have a B.S. degree in bullshitting."

Usually the bullshitting is couched as a joke. Other times Mame spins elaborate, creative fibs that seem so important to her—storytelling being her survival mechanism—that I never call her on them. She claims to have a boyfriend named Harry Zammersnak, a former U.S. congressman from Los Angeles who takes her to the theater and to posh eateries where she feasts on "muvvah-lous steak dinners" with "flamin' desserts."

"Harry is driving my cripple ass up to Mammoth [a ski resort] for the weekend," she'll say. Or, "Mister Edwards, I attended the Academy Awards last night with Harry. A very grandiose occasion. Elizabeth Taylor was there with her periwinkle-blue eyes and million-dollar diamonds. She was very despondent because Richard [Burton] didn't win the Oscar for *Anne of the Thousand Days*. They gave it instead to John Wayne for *True Grit*. Such a travesty. Why, that picture isn't even of blockbusterous proportions!"

Mame mentions Harry so regularly that one day—this is long before the internet—I spend hours at the public library searching through phone books and almanacs and the *Readers' Guide to Periodical Literature* for mentions of a former congressman by that name. Nothing turns up. Instead of the flesh-and-blood lover Mame desires and never finds, Harry is a paper moon, a fantasy. Remember Miss Lonelyhearts' phantom suitor in Hitchcock's *Rear Window* — the absent man who gets his own place setting at a candlelit dinner for two? That was Harry.

There's a longing for connection in Mame that she masks with flip, irreverent humor. It's the devil she drowns with her excessive drinking. One Christmas Eve I meet her for an early dinner—"Mele Kalikimaka" she says with a kiss on the cheek —but when I explain that I'll be spending the remainder of the evening at home with my parents and brothers she looks crushed. She was expecting a longer visit. There is no family for her to go home to.

In 1972 I move to San Francisco, but I stay in touch with Mame with occasional phone calls—"I wore out my last pair of prostheses," she reveals one day, "and donated them to the Smithsonian Institution"—and when I visit my parents in West Covina I always schedule time with her. We talk movies and music and politics, and joke about that dreary phone-soliciting gig we survived. Mostly I let her expound—encourage her, really— on whatever she wants to talk about. All these years later, she still calls me "Mister Edwards."

One afternoon I drive by Mame's new apartment in West Covina and find her entertaining two or three high school students with snacks and alcohol. "So your girlfriend, does she 'go around the world'?" she asks a callow blond jock who's starting to slur and wobble. Two more drinks and he's passed out on the stair landing. This is not good. The following year Mame tells me she's moved to North Las Vegas. No details are offered, but I have to wonder if she lost her job with the West Covina

In Las Vegas with Mamie, 1986. That's Pia Zadora at left.

Unified School District because some teenager's parent filed a complaint.

In Vegas, Mame collects welfare and tries working a personal injury claim against Coca-Cola for an alleged chipped tooth. When she asks to borrow money from me, saying she needs it to buy a funeral wreath for her mother, the terms and tone of our friendship change. A second request arrives, for several hundred dollars, and despite my father's warning that "the quickest way to lose a friend is to loan them money," I send her a check.

Over several months Mame pays off part of the loan, and then the checks stop. "Are you bitter with me?" she asks in a letter. I don't remember how I respond, only that there are never harsh words or recriminations—just the sad, gradual dimming of our friendship. One year I receive no Christmas card and my correspondence comes back with a "not at this address" stamp. I investigate online, wondering if she's died, but nothing shows up. Years pass and finally, while writing this essay, I go to the Family Search Library at the Church of Jesus Christ of Latter

Day Saints in Oakland and discover that Mame died on January 30, 2004. She was sixty.

I locate her sister Elizabeth Rice in Alabama and telephone her. "You knew Mamie Jackson!" she exclaims in her honeyed drawl. Miss Elizabeth tells me Mame died in her sleep, after going out with friends the previous evening. "I don't know," she says softly when I ask her the cause of death. Perhaps she knows and doesn't want to say. There were 12 children in the family, Elizabeth adds, all born and raised in Alabama—not in Hawaii, as Mamie liked to claim.

"She really was one of a kind," Elizabeth says with a sigh.

I haven't seen my friend in twenty years, but her humor and originality, her intelligence and language and appreciation for the absurd have never left me. Close friends have all heard my Mame stories over the years, and I still get a laugh quoting her and mimicking that buttery voice that segued so quickly from grand-lady eloquence to jaw-dropping raunch.

I raise my glass to you, Mamie. You rascal.

Chapter Fifteen
Europe on Five Dollars a Day

It seemed reasonable to me. I was about to go to Europe for three months, and if I budgeted myself correctly the trip would cost $450 for the entire summer. Ninety days.

So that's what I did. It was 1971 and I was twenty, the summer between my junior and senior years of college. I'd saved money from working in the campus library and with $450 in traveler's checks, a Eurail Pass, a copy of Arthur Frommer's *Europe on $5 a Day*, and a borrowed backpack, I boarded a charter flight from Oakland to Amsterdam.

I did it alone, because none of my friends had the money or inclination to go for that long. It didn't occur to me I'd get lonely, which I often did, or that my $5 daily stipend would prove awfully limiting and sometimes painful. I traveled rough: staying in youth hostels that charged the equivalent of $2.15 for bed and breakfast; sleeping occasionally on trains; lunching on dismal Wimpy burgers in England; eating yogurt, cheese, and a hunk of bread on a park bench and calling that dinner.

Every single American college student was tramping through Europe that summer, or so it seemed. *Time* magazine ran a story about the great exodus, with a cover photo of a longhaired coed wearing a backpack and boarding a plane. Hordes of young Europeans, Canadians and Australians were on the road, too, and

Trafalgar Square, London

what developed was a roving fraternity of young and curious, like-minded adventurers. We crossed paths, swapped stories, and shared information about bargain flights and cheap accommodations, hostels to avoid, destinations not to miss.

I slept on cement floors more than once. In Madrid, a dusty hostel on the edge of town had no toilet facilities, just holes in the floor with well-worn grooves to place your feet in. In Munich, hostelers were awakened each morning when a Wagnerian frau stomped through the dormitory banging an enormous stewpot with a heavy metal spoon. In Geneva, they blasted you awake Waco-style with loud music until you got out of bed. Most hostels required that you vacate after breakfast and barred you from re-entering until 5 p.m. or later. That kind of thing gets tiring.

I took a detour to the countryside north of Paris where my Aunt Betty and Uncle Bob were teaching at the European Bible Institute in Lamorlaye. I could catch up on sleep there and uncouple from the clang of the tourist circuit. Eat Aunt Betty's cooking, do my laundry and enjoy my aunt's quiet, graceful hospitality. I adored her.

I visited nine countries in thirteen weeks, circling counterclockwise from England and Scotland to France, Spain, Switzerland, Italy, Germany, Denmark and back to Holland. In Barcelona I was introduced to sangria, tapas, and the audacious, dripping-candle architecture of Antoni Gaudi. In Denmark I visited a tiny, remote village where two American friends were escaping the Vietnam War and apprenticing as ceramicists. After two weeks in Britain, I crossed the English Channel on a hovercraft and felt like I'd jumped from dreary black-and-white into gorgeous Technicolor when I arrived in France. Near the dock in Calais I discovered a fromagerie that sold cheeses I'd never heard of, some in huge, five-feet-tall wheels. I found a wine shop

Paris

next door, followed by a patisserie and a flower shop exploding with color and fragrance and something that felt like a celebration of life.

In Barcelona, I was hosted by Raul Alcalay, a Catalan who'd spent a year as foreign exchange student in my hometown of West Covina. On the back of Raul's motor scooter I got a tour of Barcelona and everything designed by Gaudi. His family dined at 10 p.m., a multi-course meal that lasted almost till midnight, and later Raul took me to rowdy tavernas where Catalan men played guitar and drunkenly sang Cuban revolutionary songs. At night I slept in the Alcalays' tiny guest room and felt very fortunate but also awkward. In another part of the spacious apartment Raul's lovely mother, forty-five years old at most, was dying of cancer.

In Denmark, I boarded a train in Copenhagen, located on the island of Sjaelland, and headed west. The entire locomotive rode onto a huge ferry that traversed a fourteen-mile body of water, then left the ferry and crossed overland on the island of Fyn, finally connecting to the Jutland peninsula. From Montreux, that elegant town on Lake Geneva, I took the greatest train journey of my life. As we headed east to German-speaking Switzerland, a stream of cheerful, rosy-cheeked hikers boarded wearing lederhosen and carrying rucksacks and pointed, hand-carved alpenstocks. The train kept climbing.

Taverna-hopping with Raul Alcalay and two Swiss friends of his.

The Alpine landscape grew lusher and cooler, and by late afternoon we had slowed to a crawl as the train finessed a tangle of tight curves. The scenery was so enchanted that when the train turned to reveal a waterfall magically filtered through foggy mist, everyone on the train—day hikers, old ladies, tourists and children—quietly sighed in unison. Or so it seems to me in retrospect. A perfect moment.

The train terminated in Interlaken, where the youth hostel was full. Outside the train station I met a lively Dutch family who invited me to share their dinner and spend the night at their camping site on Lake Thun. Mr. and Mrs. Van Dyk's kindness and generosity were overwhelming, and their beer excellent. When it rained buckets, their son Chris rescued me from the leaky tent they'd loaned me, and set me up on the floor of their RV. The lightning was thrilling that night. With each angry thunderbolt the entire valley lit up like high noon in July – so brightly that the peaks of the Jungfrau, the Eiger, and the Mönch stood out in sharp relief.

The following day I thanked the Van Dyks and took a narrow-gauge train on its steep ascent to Grindelwald, probably the prettiest, most pristine village I've ever visited. Rustic chalets with flower boxes at each window, the freshest air, amazing vistas. Everything sparkled. I remember speaking to a pair of old Swiss hikers who asked how long I'd be staying. When I said just one day, they looked sad for me. "Oh, you Americans. Always rushing to the next destination." My memory of Grindelwald is bittersweet, precisely because I didn't stay longer and also because I'd probably be disappointed by its growth and the clamor of tourism if I returned.

In Amsterdam, the last stop on my journey, I wandered into a record store where you could rent a turntable by the hour and

Original album cover for Joni Mitchell's transcendent *Blue*.

listen to a brand-new LP. I chose Joni Mitchell's new release, *Blue*, and instantly fell in love. The songs on that album—intimate, deeply revealing—were written during Joni's extended European gadabout and they capture the experience of being young and yearning and on the move. The song "California," with its plaintive longing for home and connection, sounded like it was written for me. I'm sure a lot of people felt that way, and still do.

Still a lot of lands to see
But I wouldn't wanna stay here
It's too old and cold and settled in its ways here

Oh, but California
Cal-i-for-nia!, I'm coming home...

The ten songs on *Blue* last only thirty-six minutes, but they're so textured and resonant, and so beautifully sequenced, that you feel as you might after reading a rich and satisfying novel. I love Joni's voice, her melodies, the way her lyrics find their musical equivalents in spare arrangements for piano, acoustic guitar, and dulcimer. So much of what I felt that summer in Europe is distilled on that record. The day after hearing *Blue* for the first time—to this day, it's still my favorite album—I flew home to California.

That summer in Europe was the beginning of a lifetime of travel—a passion that's never sated. I don't travel rough any longer, and sometimes I spend as much money in three days (not allowing for inflation) as I spent over three months in 1971. I've visited forty-five countries and all seven continents and as I write this I'm impatient, waiting for COVID to vanish to the point where I can explore again without hesitation.

Travel teaches you a lot: geography and history, other languages and cultures; how to see the world through another's eyes; how to think openly and curiously and without a nationalist bias.

Chapter Sixteen

San Francisco 1972:
A Dive in the Deep End

S an Francisco didn't welcome me with a warm embrace and a bottle of beer. The second I drove through the Golden Gate Bridge toll booth, a cop pulled me over and cited me for a smoking vehicle violation. Within a week, I'd also received my first parking ticket and had my car towed and impounded.

After the warm cocoon of Arcata, San Francisco felt cold and harsh. People were abrupt and suspicious. They drove too fast. One day I asked a Muni bus driver if he could wait a second while I went inside a corner store to get change for bus fare. He laughed at my naiveté and drove on—but in a town like Arcata that request wouldn't have been unusual. When I told that story to my first San Francisco friend, he laughed and called me a bumpkin.

I was twenty-one when I arrived. I approached San Francisco as an experiment, a way station to something bigger that I couldn't yet formulate. I'd graduated from Humboldt State in June 1972, and during the summer that followed—a strange limbo between protection and independence—I came out as gay to one of my housemates and she in turn came out to me. Paula had friends in San Francisco, and when they invited us to share their flat in the Haight Ashbury district, we loaded our belongings into the 1963 Chevy Nova station wagon I'd just

My first San Francisco address, 603 Clayton Street, was one short block from this legendary street corner.

bought for $50. From the moment we got the invitation until we drove away from Arcata, only six days had passed. Such are the mobility and disinhibition of youth.

I hadn't lived in a city since I was a small boy in Chicago, and I wanted to explore my sexuality and the cultural opportunities of a major urban setting. But Haight Street, five years after the Summer of Love, had lost its festive, friendly-village vibe and bore the scars of heroin and speed traffic. Sidewalks were littered with dog crap, and longtime residents were wary and exhausted from the hippie invasion and its jangly aftermath.

And yet, we were in San Francisco. Paula and I lived at 603 Clayton, at the corner of Haight. The flat was a bit dismal and noisy, and five months later I found my own apartment two blocks away on Oak Street, in a pink stucco building facing the Panhandle. Downstairs lived two gay brothers from Vermont, Ray the dancer and Dann the mime, with their rowdy parrot Peckerhead. On the first floor two Russian widows, Mrs. Ikonokoff and Mrs. Poltoratskaya, kept an anxious vigil with their nervous cats. There weren't many vestiges of pre-hippie days still remaining in 1973, but amidst the anarchist bookstore and the head shops on Haight Street you found a Russian bakery that sold delectable baklava and piroshki; a Chinese grocery where the butcher cheerfully complained, "Work never end!"; a used-furniture store run by Holocaust survivors; and the Persian Aub Zam Zam, a smoke-stained bar where the surly Assyrian proprietor gave you the boot if he didn't respect your drink order.

Nobody in San Francisco had any money—not in my milieu, anyway—but nobody seemed depressed about it. I met a struggling gospel pianist, Bobby Kent, who threw himself a rent party where guests brought cheap wine and dropped coins and dollar bills into a large goldfish bowl. We decorated our apartments with thrift-shop furniture, old movie posters and houseplants— philodendrons, maidenhair ferns and hardy coleuses—and built bookcases from cinder blocks and scavenged boards. My desk was an old door I found on the street, balanced over matching nightstands. I slept on the floor on a secondhand mattress and box spring and used my freshly laundered T-shirts and underwear as extra pillows. It didn't seem strange at the time.

City life was amazingly cheap: bus fare was 25 cents, my rent share $85. Half the people I knew didn't work. Why bother, when food stamps and public assistance were so accessible? It was easy to get ATD (Aid to the Totally Disabled), a type of welfare that hippie scammers called "crazy money." All you had to do was shave your eyebrows, stay up all night before your appointment, and perform a reasonable simulation of derangement before the burned-out intake worker judged you unfit for employment.

Bearded and long-haired in San Francisco, 1974.

At 1959 Oak Street I advertised for a roommate and the first person who answered was Rob Jerome, a close friend to this day. We shared a sense of humor and a passion for language, movies and pop culture. We made weekly pilgrimages to the Stud, the greatest gay bar that ever existed. It was located South of Market and got its name because it started as a leather bar. By the time I arrived in 1972, it was a buoyant, Dionysian dream of beautiful long-haired hippie men and their friends. The crowd was celebratory and the decor festive with muted lighting, dozens of candles and a tiny electric train that circled the top of an oval-shaped bar. The Stud had a house DJ and his music was sensational: I still can't hear the Temptations' "Papa Was a Rolling Stone," David Bowie's "Suffragette City" or anything from the Rolling Stones' *Exile on Main Street* without a giddy, blood-rushing flashback to the Stud's crackling energy.

Across the street on Folsom was Hamburger Mary's, a diner where the hostess Heidi was a Jean Harlow look-alike who dished out big-sister love to young gay guys. The half-and-half for your coffee came in baby bottles with the top of the nipple snipped off, and the walls were covered with household junk, campy ephemera and framed photos of Hollywood glamour queens Marlene Dietrich and Joan Crawford. Quaaludes were big, and one of the regulars was a druggie named Karla who was "luded" every night. "Karla, how are you?" I asked one night outside Hamburger Mary's. "Ohhh, totally fucked up," she slurred, struggling not to topple onto the sidewalk in her platform shoes. To me, "fucked up" meant emotionally distraught, not bombed out of your head. So when I offered a sympathetic "Gee, I'm sorry," she looked at me like I was nuts.

Rob and I loved the Stud and Hamburger Mary's and observed the regulars so often that we concocted nicknames for them with corresponding mythologies. Untouchable. Still Waters. Mr. Perfect. Adenoid Annie. David the Drag Queen was another fixture, a hapless soul who cadged his drag from second-hand bins but had no concept of what looked good on him. A halter top and electric-blue satin hot pants one night, a tattered negligee the next, a Little Bo Peep outfit for Halloween. He had eyeglasses

Great music, great atmosphere. Dionysian dream.

Hamburger Mary's, 1980. *Photo by Janet Delaney.*

with thick lenses and a waiflike, stumbling-through-life mien. Most of the guys at the Stud wore denim jeans and flannel shirts and projected a woodsy masculinity that David couldn't simulate for the life of him. Today, he'd identify as transgender or non-binary and use neutral pronouns. He'd have a community of kindred souls. Back then he was a tiny minority within a minority.

When the Stud closed at 2 a.m., we might grab a few stragglers and share a taxi to The Haven, an all-night restaurant on Polk Street that made smoothies and crunchy wheat-berry sandwiches with alfalfa sprouts. You might feel out of place if you weren't tripping on cocaine or speed, but the coalescence of drag queens, druggies, longhaired Adonises and street kids made for great theater. It was Max's Kansas City with a California twist.

If you haunted The Haven during the daytime you'd glimpse Jesus Christ Satan, a middle-aged satyr who stood on the sidewalk waving his United Nations flag. "J.C.," as friends called him, was an unglued, grinning exhibitionist, and one night he rushed the stage at an Angels of Light performance, ripped off his clothes, and snorted amyl nitrate before he got the hook.

The Angels were an offshoot of the Cockettes, a notorious tribe of bearded drag queens and merry lunatics who capered at the Palace Theatre in North Beach. They were legendary, and when I was brand new in town Bobby Kent took me to a Cockettes midnight show on Halloween. Someone took our picture in the audience as we waited for the show to begin, me in a beat-up vintage suit, Bobby in his enormous, reddish-blond Afro. A week later I opened *Rolling Stone* and there we were. The photographer who captured us was the soon-to-be-famous Annie Leibovitz.

The show was *Vice Palace* and the stars were Divine, the 300-pound star of John Waters's *Pink Flamingos,* and Goldie Glitters, a six-foot-two, snaggle-toothed queen who later played the title role in *Cinderella.* Two long-haired

The stars of Vice Palace. Divine at center. *Photo by Clay Geerdes with permission by David Miller.*

hunks performed a naked pas de deux. Goldie Glitters made a fabulous mincing entrance, struck a camp pose with hand on hip and declared, to thunderous laughter, "My girdle's too tight and my cunt is killing me!" Mink Stole sang "No Nose Nanook" and a line of tap dancers came out dressed as Eskimos. More shrieking from the audience, more hollering and stomping.

How to convey the volcanic energy and joy in that room? The roar was so loud—it had a physical presence, a rumble, a thrust—that some of the dancers started to wobble and lose their balance. I vividly remember a young woman at the end of the tap line with an ecstatic, blissed-out grin. If she wasn't high already, the audience made her high. I've never seen a performer/audience reciprocity so electric.

Drugs fueled the mad, unrestrained hippie roar in the Palace Theater, as did a rush of long-repressed spirit, sexuality and creativity. We were the children of the 1950s, misfits and outsiders, mostly gay, raised in a rigid conformity that scorned differentness. We were eager to blossom, thrilled to find an affinity group and committed to shedding the itchy frogskin of shame and secrecy.

The excitement that the Cockettes conjured on stage—their tawdry glamour and anarchistic glee—were emblematic of the San Francisco I discovered that year. All that divine decadence entertained and thrilled me up to a point—it was so unlike anything I'd known—but ultimately, as I yearned for a community, the scene exhausted me and made me feel alone. It was all too fast, too frenzied and voracious. The easy sex and hedonism of the 1970s, that decade between the Stonewall Riots and AIDS, didn't foster intimacy. They complicated and sometimes thwarted it. Sexual compulsion works that way: there's always a brighter candle around the next corner, a flower more fragrant, an intrigue as yet unexplored. It makes a person feel disposable.

———◆———

After two and a half years I left San Francisco and moved to Berkeley, where my best friends Rob and April were living. I needed something slower and quieter, less congested. I found a studio apartment above a garage on Derby Street. I liked being close to San Francisco, connected by the F bus that crossed the Bay Bridge, but I couldn't handle being inside the vortex. A decade later I bought a house in the Rockridge neighborhood of Oakland, where I live today on a leafy street in a 1912 Craftsman-style bungalow. The East Bay gave me a happy medium between the cultural vitality and pulse of the city, and the less frantic rhythms and warmth I felt in Arcata. I still feel that way today.

Chapter Seventeen
San Francisco: Working

U nlike a lot of people I knew in San Francisco, I worked. Days after arriving in the city, I answered a classified ad in the *San Francisco Chronicle* for a print shop needing a typesetter and paste-up artist. I got the job—two dollars an hour—and commuted each day to Brisbane, a tiny, hillside town south of San Francisco. A married couple, Fred and Francine Holder, had converted the lower floor of their house into an office and darkroom and installed a printing press in their garage.

The Holders were in their late twenties but their cynical, hard-knocks crust made them seem much older. Fred was the nicer of the two. Francine was a bully and an emotional cyclone. Each day I arrived early, swept the floor, and made coffee before a grumbling Francine trudged downstairs and began her daily routine of chain-smoking, coughing, schmoozing the customers, and chewing out the paper and ink vendors on the phone.

She was smart as a devil but bitter and conditioned by early wounds to see the world as a cruel force organized to cheat and demean her. Francine's nerves were especially raw that autumn because she'd just come off primal therapy, a trendy alternative to talk therapy that required the client to dredge up repressed childhood trauma with hysterical screaming and beating on pillows.

"It's a bitch of a therapy," Francine said, in a tone that was half exhausted and half boastful. Her problems started at age four, when her birth parents arranged to keep two of their children and relinquish the other two, Francine included, to an adoption agency. Their abandonment haunted and defined her life.

Francine had seven-year-old twins from her first marriage—mini-versions of herself, with sour dispositions—and a bubbly two-year-old daughter with Fred. To her face Fred was jolly, but behind Francine's back he complained about her mood swings, cutting language, and mow-them-down urge for control. Francine didn't spare me, either: She called me "the kid" and blamed her mistakes on me.

Such an odd pair. Fred: short, reddish-blond with a goatee and scrappy bantam quality that was mostly bluster. Francine: taller, a lot heavier, with a husky voice and physical heft that she exploited to intimidate people. She wore her hair pulled back into a ponytail and dressed in dull, nondescript clothes. Usually black or gray. "I know I look like a butch dyke," she observed.

The work we did, typesetting and paste-up, were the conventional production modes in those years before computer graphics. We created display ads; flyers and business forms; restaurant menus and table tents, an industry term for table-top triangles promoting specials and house wines. For business forms I stood over a light table and ruled all the lines by hand with Rapidograph technical pens. Once the form was ruled, I'd slip it through the platen of an IBM Selectric composer and type the column headings in six- or eight-point type in tiny boxes. If I needed an extra-large font at the top of the form, I grabbed a sheet of Letraset press type and rubbed down, character by character. By today's standards, those practices were primitive. Mortar and pestle.

Typesetting on an IBM Selectric. In the Dark Ages, before computer graphics.

Downstairs in the garage, Fred's younger brother, a recently discharged Vietnam veteran, ran the printing press and erupted daily in volcanic torrents of cursing when the press malfunctioned. Francine rolled her eyes, lit another cigarette, and sighed. Each night I'd go home and furnish my flatmates with the latest lurid chapter of the Fred and Francine soap opera. They were always entertained.

At 3 p.m. each day, Francine's world-weary twins would stumble in after school. "I'm bored," Emily whined one afternoon. "There's nothing to do."

"Well," Francine responded with a jaded yawn, "you could watch the moss grow on my twat."

Verbatim. To a seven-year-old. You never knew what she might say or do, only that it would probably scorch the earth. So when Francine vanished one day, having learned that Fred was canoodling with another woman, her abrupt departure wasn't out of character. She closed the bank accounts, and in a puff of smoke took the girls with her in the station wagon. Fred had no idea where she'd gone, but aside from missing his youngest, Suzie, he was downright giddy and wished Francine good riddance—a sentiment echoed by several customers.

Almost immediately, Fred's hapless girlfriend Debbie— picture Mrs. Wiggins, the big-bottomed secretary on *The Carol Burnett Show*—claimed Francine's desk. She answered the phone, stole hugs and kisses from Fred, and promised the customers that Francine the gorgon was gone, really gone for good.

A divorce attorney was engaged, and on his advice Fred prepared physical evidence of Francine's rank performance as mother and housekeeper. He took stark black-and-white photos of dirty dishes sitting in the sink, images that resembled the classic Weegee photos of New York car crashes and murder victims. He photographed the filthy bathroom and unkempt bedrooms; the parched, needleless pine tree that still stood, covered in tinsel, a full three months after Christmas. Apparently, Fred didn't take into account that Francine managed the print shop and worked as hard as he did, and was therefore no more responsible for household maintenance than he.

Two weeks after her disappearance, Francine suddenly rematerialized with daughters in tow. No explanation. I came to work and there she was—mounted like a commanding officer at the same desk where Debbie, presumably dismissed, had so briefly, faithfully, and aspirationally sat. No talk of divorce, no more Weegee-like evidence of domestic neglect. Never a word uttered about the rift, where Francine had spent her mystery fortnight, or how Fred had rejoiced in her absence.

After nine months I'd grown tired of Francine's foul moods

and the long commute from San Francisco. But when I gave two weeks' notice she ordered me to leave immediately. After the months she'd spent training me, she said, she couldn't bear to see my ungrateful self. Unemployment insurance followed, along with a cool, bracing wave of relief. It's important to know when to walk away—when to grow up and respect yourself. I wish I'd done that kind of thing a lot more when I was young.

The Storybook Theater company: Ray Houle, Kate MacLaren, me, Dann Houle.

One day, some thirty years after leaving the dysfunctional Holders, I called Fred's brother Vince and asked whatever had happened to Fred and Francine. I had no motive, just curiosity and an appreciation for good stories. Vince was circumspect and gave non-answers to all my questions. I'm sure I wasn't the first person to call him for information on his brother and sister-in-law. He probably took me for an IRS agent or disgruntled creditor.

———•———

After the Holders, I scooped ice cream one summer at Old Uncle Gaylord's in North Beach (loved their rum raisin), found another paste-up and typesetting job in San Francisco, and scored a weekend acting gig with a children's theater company. The entrepreneur of Storybook Theater was Arthur Meyer, a middle-aged eccentric who also managed Carol Doda, the legendary San Francisco stripper. Carol pioneered topless dancing in the late 1960s and famously augmented her breasts with silicone injections, blooming from a modest size 32 to a jolly, money-making size 44. Arthur also directed Ms. Doda in a stage revival of W. Somerset Maugham's *Rain* and a long-forgotten movie, *The Rise and Fall of the World (As Seen from a Sexual Position)*.

Arthur's leap from sexploitation to kiddie entertainment seemed strange, but in fact both enterprises were driven by his anything-for-a-buck ambition. Arthur projected a breezy daffiness reminiscent of *Match Game* regular Charles Nelson Reilly.

In our papier-mâché *Peter Rabbit* heads, which were horribly uncomfortable with exposed chicken wire inside. "Uncle Arthur" guides us here to another shopping mall audience.

Just below that persona was a wily hustler with bills to pay, a surfeit of chutzpah and a modicum of talent.

We actors were horribly underpaid—$25 each for an entire weekend—but we had fun performing at county fairs and shopping malls. There were four of us in the company: me, the brothers Ray and Dann who lived in the apartment below me on Oak Street, and a spirited motorcyclist named Kate, whom Arthur dubbed "the chick." I wasn't happy that he called me "Mr. Ed," the name of a TV sitcom with a talking horse. The four actors called him "Uncle Arthur."

I played the King in *Sleeping Beauty* and wore huge papier-mâché heads as the Big Bad Wolf in *Three Little Pigs* and Mother Rabbit in *Peter Rabbit*. We all did double- and triple-duty as roadies and grunts. Unloaded the van, assembled the sets, struck the sets at the end of a gig and reloaded the van. Sometimes our paychecks bounced. At twenty-two you're game for just about anything.

———◆———

All the time I was typesetting, scooping ice cream and cavorting on stages in papier-mâché heads, I had the nagging feeling I should be using my journalism degree. The sticking point was that newspaper writing, at least the way it was presented at Humboldt State, didn't inspire me. I was a product of the late 1960s, drawn to openness and innovation, and the old-school journalistic mandates of objectivity and keeping yourself out of the story left me cold. It was formulaic and constricting, a world apart from the New Journalism of Hunter S. Thompson, Joan Didion, and Tom Wolfe, to which I aspired. I wanted to capture the cultural dynamism of the early 1970s—not as it might appear to a neutral newsperson, but to someone immersed in it. I remember reading a quote from Ken Kesey that captured my conundrum perfectly: "I'd rather be a lightning rod than a seismograph."

That's why I didn't apply for a newspaper job when I graduated from college. I'd spent my life in classrooms and I knew I lacked the maturity, confidence and life experience to start interpreting the world for others. I was still a kid. I also had the luxury of indecision: in the early 1970s we didn't have the financial pressure, the red-hot imperative to immediately launch a career that college graduates face today. Among my peers, at least, financial security wasn't as urgent as finding your bliss and means of expression. So different from today.

Gradually, the itch to tell stories came back to me. "I *am* a writer," I told myself. "This is what I'm meant to do and need to do." In 1975 I became a full-time freelancer. I drew $52 a week in unemployment insurance and paid $130 a month for a studio apartment above a garage in south Berkeley. Me, my manual typewriter and a drip coffee maker. As rejection slips mounted, I went back to graphic arts to supplement my writing income. My weekly theater reviews in the *Berkeley Gazette* brought $25 apiece. It took many years but ultimately, on the strength of several freelance pieces, the *San Francisco Chronicle* hired me as a staff writer in January 1984. I remained there another twenty-five years.

Chapter Eighteen
I Ask a Lot of Questions

I was born curious. Since I was very young, I've always asked a lot of questions. Occasionally I overdo it. Some people are flattered when you ask them about their lives, but others consider it an unwelcome breach of personal boundaries.

"I see the journalist coming out in you," they say. Actually, it's the other way around. Curiosity was intrinsic to me and journalism, which indulged, legitimized and sharpened my curiosity, was the result. I've interviewed and written about people from all walks of life, from safecrackers to sex surrogates, goat ranchers to longshoremen, but the ones who got the most attention and left me with the juiciest anecdotes were celebrities.

My favorites were the luminaries I'd admired all my life, like Lucille Ball and Gregory Peck. I met silent-screen legend Lillian Gish when she was close to ninety, handed her a single-stemmed red rose and kissed her on her cheek. It felt as soft as a rose petal. Tap dancer Ann Miller, girlish and naïve and exuding old-school glamour, gave me such a good interview, with so many luscious quotes ("She had legs from hell to breakfast"), that the *San Francisco Chronicle* elevated me from freelancer to staff writer. Thanks, Annie.

Mary Martin, so magical in *Peter Pan*, was adorable. Like Lucy and Ann Miller, she made me feel like a favored nephew.

With the delightful Ann Miller. She was touring in the stage musical *Sugar Babies*.

Esther Williams, who'd written a bawdy, tell-all memoir, was a kick in the pants, but when I asked if she still swam in her pool every day she groaned and said, "Oh Edward, now you're just entertaining yourself." Debbie Reynolds was dear, but I could see she felt lonely by herself in a huge Nob Hill hotel suite. Her daughter Carrie Fisher's second marriage had just ended, and the way she spoke about it illustrated the link they shared: a symbiosis so strong that when Carrie fell off the wagon or lost another relationship—or, ultimately, when she died—her mother suffered in tandem with her.

———— • ————

Sometimes my interviews took place in the celebrity's home, sometimes on a film location but most often in a hotel where a publicist or personal assistant hovered on the periphery. In most cases, the interviewee was promoting a movie, book, TV show, or theater production.

I think I'm a good interviewer, mostly because I'm genuinely interested and I listen well. You can't fake interest; it looks bad if you try. Also, I'm a major movie fan, so in most cases I was more than happy meeting movie stars and filmmakers. Curiosity and enthusiasm aren't the whole picture, though. You need skills as an interviewer. Like letting your subject finish a thought before jumping in with a new question. Like maintaining eye contact, concentrating on every word the person says and rarely talking about yourself. Like striking a tone that's conversational and informal, and keeping your questions short and specific.

———◆———

When I tell people I interviewed celebrities for a living they often ask, "Who were the worst?" Scoundrels and creeps make the best copy, and hearing about the bad manners of the rich and famous satisfies our desire for schadenfreude. It reminds us we're all deeply flawed—albeit in most cases lucky enough not to be publicly exposed as such.

Robert De Niro is notorious among journalists as a grouchy interview subject. I think he cultivates that reputation. Still, I felt hopeful the day I met him, since we were about to discuss his late father—and not the younger De Niro's movie career. Robert De Niro Sr. (1922-1993) was an abstract-expressionist painter, and in 1998 a San Francisco art gallery mounted a retrospective of his work. De Niro agreed to attend the opening, so wouldn't he welcome a chance to honor his gifted father?

Not really. Instead of warming to the subject, De Niro was peevish and reactive, like the grumpy grandpas he plays on screen. He sat with the gallery owner, who may have been as in-

Interviewing Robert De Niro. Never again.

timidated as I was. I asked about his early memories of his father, who separated from Bobby's mother when their son was two; about seeing his father at work; about his thoughts on the old man's paintings and how those thoughts changed over the years. To each question De Niro gave a curt response, often sighing, as if I were a penance to be endured. The more grudging and monosyllabic he was, the more uncomfortable I became. Finally, after one question he particularly didn't like, De Niro looked at the gallerist and lifted his hands, palms up, as if to say, "Y'see what crap I have to deal with?"

Others were difficult in different ways. Rex Harrison, whose swank apartment was located in the same Upper East Side building as Greta Garbo's, was imperious and stingingly condescending, exactly like—or maybe worse than—his Henry Higgins character in *My Fair Lady*. Michael Douglas seemed to think my function as interviewer was to fawn over him, and resented questions about movies he made that didn't turn out well. And

John Cusack, plagued with interview fatigue and adolescent petulance, refused to make eye contact and spoke so faintly that my recorder didn't pick up a word.

————◆————

It's inevitable you won't hit it off with everyone. Maybe it's your mistake: you assume an unwelcome familiarity, dig too deep, or make a clumsy joke. You might discover you have nothing in common with the person and no attempt to manufacture chemistry will suffice. Or (see Cusack), your subject is saddled with back-to-back interviews and what you encounter is an exhausted shell.

When Laurie Metcalf was in San Francisco to do a play at American Conservatory Theatre, she postponed and rescheduled our interview three times the morning we were set to meet. When we finally sat down to talk, she multitasked, autographing a stack of eight-by-ten-inch glossies of herself as she spoke. When I asked Roz Chast, the New Yorker cartoonist, "Could you paint me a verbal picture of your family and yourself at twelve years old?" she said, "Why don't you just talk to my shrink?" And when I interviewed a self-satisfied, nineteen-year-old Helena Bonham Carter in the year *A Room with a View* made her a star, she lifted her patrician chin and opined that entertainment journalists "are all parasitic, basically."

Remember Jesse Ventura, the professional wrestler who made a few movies and became governor of Minnesota in a freak election victory? I interviewed him in 1987, when he co-starred with Arnold Schwarzenegger in the movie *Predator*. Arnold, who hadn't gone into politics yet, was a gentleman. Jesse was not. When I asked if pro wrestling is mostly staged and rehearsed —"fake" was the word I used—he glared at me and threatened,

"Well, I could pick you up and give you a body slam. Then you could tell me how fake it is."

———— ♦ ————

I usually held my own in a celebrity interview, but when I spoke with the legendary singer and pianist Nina Simone, her anger frightened me. She called from a pay telephone on a busy street in Los Angeles, which right away seemed strange, and wanted to know if she would be paid for the interview. *No, sorry.* Then she ordered me to arrange a Brink's bodyguard for her, which I didn't know how to do and didn't think, as a journalist, I should do. Doesn't Brink's transport money in armored trucks, instead of providing bodyguards for celebrities?

With Arnold Schwarzenegger. "Watch that cigar, please."

Nina Simone. *Photo by Ron Kroon.*

I tried to get a rhythm going with Simone but every question brought a volatile response. Yes, she said, she was still fighting record companies: "Honey, I'll be in litigation over royalties and monies owed me until I die!" And yes, she was estranged from her only child and grandson: "I don't see either one of them. So as far as I'm concerned, I don't have a daughter Lisa. That's good enough for me!"

She was a raw, open wound. For Simone—who fought discrimination all her life and lived for fifteen years in Africa and Europe to escape American racism; who bore overwhelming bitterness and sorrow despite her acclaim—those responses were totally in character. She once fired a gun at a record company executive to demand unpaid royalties, was arrested in France for shooting an air gun at a neighbor's rowdy child, and had a history of berating audiences and canceling concerts at the last minute. Years after her death, I read she'd been diagnosed with bipolar disorder and prescribed the antipsychotic drug Trilafon. Had she gone off her meds the day we spoke? Possibly.

Finally, when I told her I was doing the interview because I loved her music, and not because the story was assigned to me, Ms. Simone cut me off. "Love me, my ass!" she shouted into the phone. "I need somebody to protect me and I asked you about a Brink's bodyguard. I don't want no chokin' kind of love, sir! It ain't never fed me and it ain't never took care of me."

Nina Simone died in 2003, at seventy. I saw her in concert three times and when she was on her game, she was exquisite. Her voice was searing, mighty; a moan from her was greater than all the fuss and theatrics of any dozen other performers. She played the piano brilliantly, made your body tingle with aliveness. I hope she found a modicum of peace later in life, or maybe in the sweet hereafter if that truly exists. A place to rest her scarred and broken heart.

———◆———

Luckily, most celebrity encounters were cordial. On the best occasions, they opened a window into that person's humanity. Tom Hanks and Steven Spielberg were both terrific interviews, for similar reasons. Hanks was starring in *Philadelphia*, playing a gay man dying of AIDS, and in that same year Spielberg delivered *Schindler's List*, a Holocaust story that reconnected him to his Jewish roots. Both men, stirred by the making of their respective films, were receptive and eloquent when I spoke with them.

Hanks had never done a dramatic role prior to *Philadelphia*, and the reactions to his performance were "unlike anything that I've ever come across," he told me. "At first I'd have people come up to me in restaurants and say, 'Thank you so much for what you're doing.' On the one hand that makes me feel wonderful. That's what you always want as an actor."

He paused and I saw his lower lip trembling; he was starting to cry. "But when they say, 'Thank you' I feel like it's not fair that a guy like me—who does this for a living and for fun, and a degree of glory or applause—should be given credit for faking something that [in real life] is completely final."

I met Spielberg at his spacious, adobe-style office complex at Universal Studios. After colossal success with adventure yarns and family fare (*Jaws, Indiana Jones and the Temple of Doom*), he was eager to try his hand at serious drama with the tale of Oskar Schindler, a Nazi war profiteer who saved more than 1,100 Jews from death camps. Growing up Jewish in an all-gentile section of Scottsdale, Arizona, Spielberg had viewed his ethnicity as a *shonda* (shame) and longed to assimilate. Shortly before *Schindler's,* he went back to Hebrew school with his second wife, Kate Capshaw, and learned more about his heritage in one year, he said, than in all the Jewish training of his youth. The *Schindler's* experience left him depleted, but also gave him a new life.

"So it's like a postpartum depression," I offered, "combined with an extremely profound, life-changing experience."

"Exactly," Spielberg said. "When you say those words, they sound noble. When I say those words, I feel like I'm sounding pretentious. So I've not made that statement to anybody in the press, even though what you said is true."

———◦———

Brian Wilson, the Beach Boys founder and songwriting genius, was awkward and jittery when I met him at his Mulholland Drive home. After just ten minutes of talk he stood up and bolted from the room. When he returned a minute or two later, he was cursing. "What's wrong?" I asked. "I've had a couple bad hardships," Wilson said, "and I'm all fucked up in my head. Lost my dad, lost my brother, almost lost myself, which is even more ridiculous."

He wriggled in his chair, finished his Diet Coke, belched, and left the room a second time. "Thank you very much," he said. "Talk to my wife for a while. Make her feel good."

Wilson, who spent more than a decade under the influence of sham psychotherapist Eugene Landy, was free of that ordeal at the time I met him and newly married to a wonderful woman named Melinda Ledbetter. They met when she sold him a car at a Cadillac dealership, and she saved his life. In the biographical movie *Love and Mercy* she was played to perfection by Elizabeth Banks.

"Brian suffers from depression," Ledbetter told me. "It came on in his early twenties. It'll be something he has to deal with the rest of his life." She said he was taking Zoloft, an antidepressant, and Clorazil to silence the voices and auditory hallucinations in his head. We spoke a long time, and in the next room I could hear her husband start to play his grand piano and sing. His voice, so hesitant and raspy in conversation with a stranger, was suddenly pure and clear.

———◆———

I was apprehensive when asked to do a live, on-stage interview with Faye Dunaway for the City Arts & Lectures series in San Francisco. She has a reputation for being difficult, so I didn't know what might transpire. Dunaway was promoting her memoir, *Looking for Gatsby: My Life,* and when we met in the car that drove us to the Herbst Theater in San Francisco, she asked

What's not to love about Dolly Parton? She was promoting the movie *Straight Talk*, 1992.

to see my questions in advance. I took a deep breath—this was way out of the ordinary—and said we'd fare better if she responded in the moment, unrehearsed. I didn't want her vetoing questions and staging the interview.

Faye insisted, saying she'd feel more comfortable if she could study the questions first. I knew how diva-like and intransigent she could be, so I figured I should acquiesce to avoid friction on stage. Off she went to prepare in a private room, which turned out to be a brilliant decision. I was grateful she held firm, because once we were on stage her answers were warm, detailed, and insightful. She made it all seem off-the-cuff, never letting on that she'd studied the questions in advance—she's that good an actress. We clicked beautifully, in rhythm, like a pair of dance partners sparking the best in each other. We were "in the zone." I loved it.

———◆———

I sometimes fantasize about a dream dinner party, where I'd gather all the interview subjects I've connected with most strongly. Laura Dern tops my list. I met her when she was nineteen and promoting the movie *Smooth Talk,* and interviewed her three or four times subsequently. Effervescent Laura, of all the celebrities I've encountered, is the one I would most like to have kept as a friend. I'd invite brilliant and hilarious Emma Thompson; Sarah Jessica Parker with her terrific gift of gab; and Dolly Parton, who's every bit as adorable and down-to-earth as you'd imagine.

I felt a special frisson with each of those artists. But, as I was often reminded, there's a distinct line between feeling simpatico on the one hand, and the limited, transactional nature of a press interview on the other. It's important to respect that division, which is easier said than done. Interviews are a lot like first dates: when you discover a mutual interest and rapport you want that to continue. Several famous marriages were launched with an interview: John F. Kennedy and one-time press photographer Jacqueline Bouvier Kennedy; Gregory Peck and French journalist Veronique Passani; Marlo Thomas and Phil Donahue; Clint Eastwood and news anchor Dina Ruiz.

When you make a strong connection you feel great, the same as you do with any new friendship or a budding romance. And if circumstances dictate a hasty goodbye, you feel a loss. "It is always painful to part from people whom one has known for a brief space of time," Oscar Wilde wrote in *The Importance of Being Earnest.* "The absence of old friends one can endure with equanimity, but even a momentary separation from anyone to whom one has just been introduced is almost unbearable."

That's a classic Wildean epigram. Arch and frivolous on the surface, but underneath it lies a pearl of truth.

Chapter Nineteen

My Afternoon with Lucy

I'd heard how tough and intimidating Lucille Ball could be, but on the day we met at her Beverly Hills home, four years before she died, she was warm and unguarded and down-to-earth. It felt like hanging out with a favorite aunt. She picked up quickly that I was a fan, and I think since I was young and eager she liked and trusted me.

Lucy was promoting *Stone Pillow*, a CBS TV-movie that had her playing a spunky New York City bag lady named Florabelle. Sound like a bad idea? Was it ever. Lucy was sorely miscast, but the movie's release afforded me a golden opportunity to meet a childhood idol.

Arranging the interview was surprisingly easy. One morning I called veteran CBS publicist Axel Peterson and said, "Do you think Lucy would do a one-on-one for *Stone Pillow*? I could fly down to Los Angeles." With a big star like Lucy, you'd normally get "Not a chance" or an evasive "Let me get back to you." Instead, Axel put me on hold, and in two or three minutes he was back. "Lucy wants to do it."

That kind of thing *never* happens.

I flew into Burbank on the morning of October 23, 1985, rented a car, and picked up a large, exotic floral bouquet en route to Lucy's house. I rang the doorbell at 1000 North Roxbury Drive, an assistant answered, and within seconds Lucy entered the foyer behind him. "Thank you," she said, nodding her head in a slightly regal manner. "That's a lovely bouquet." She was accustomed to deference and special treatment.

The assistant guided us into a section of the living room where Lucy and I sat and talked for nearly two hours. She wore white pants, a pleated white blouse, and turquoise-blue jacket. Tinted, oversize eyeglasses. Her hair was colored the familiar henna-red I knew from television. She was seventy-four.

Lucy's ranch-style house was comfortable and tidy, not ostentatious. No major art pieces; just a pedestrian painting of her husband, Gary Morton, swinging a golf club. In an adjoining room I spied a backgammon table, where Lucy spent hundreds of lively and competitive hours, backgammon being her favorite pastime. We weren't alone as we confabulated. Joining us was a very old man, a minder I guess you'd call him, whom CBS had sent to monitor Lucy's remarks and make sure she said nothing reckless or off-color.

Lucy was fascinated by my name. "Ed Guthmann? That's such an old man's name for a young kid like you," she said with gusto. "Lucy," I said, "I'll be thirty-five in three days," thinking I was now middle-aged. "Big deal!" she harrumphed, rolling her eyes. "Big deal!"

She reminisced about the *I Love Lucy* days, praised her ex-husband Desi Arnaz for his professional acumen ("innovation after innovation") but slammed his gambling, drinking, and womanizing ("We had five homes, but to him they were just houses"). She gave excellent marks to her current husband, comic-turned-manager Morton ("On a scale of 1 to 10 we're a 12"); and said she didn't act for five years after Vivian Vance, who played Ethel Mertz on *I Love Lucy*, died in 1979. When I

With Lucy in her Beverly Hills home.

asked how it felt to be at leisure after shooting *Stone Pillow*, she shrugged. "To tell ya the truth, it's been kinda boring around here lately!"

She didn't mince words. Lucy was at a point in her life when she had no interest in anything but the unvarnished truth, which is precisely why the ancient minder was warming up his end of the sofa.

Lucy told me she got that low, husky voice by yelling from her car on the Pacific Coast Highway, a practice that movie director Howard Hawks recommended to deepen her tone. And she grew nostalgic when I asked about her friend Clark Gable. "We used to tool around in his jeep," she said, remembering when San Fernando Valley was all farms and ranches and open land. "Oh boy," she sighed, shaking her head and looking off to one side. The image seemed to evoke thoughts of distant youth and too few friends left to share those memories.

I asked about Elizabeth Patterson, the fragile-looking character actress who played the babysitter Mrs. Trumbull on *I Love Lucy*. Lucy said Patterson took the bus home each day after taping at Desilu Studios, and never accepted invitations to socialize —not from lack of interest, but from feeling she didn't belong. She was just as modest as the characters she played.

I told Lucy I'd admired Patterson in Hollywood classics and described a poignant scene from 1940's *Remember the Night*, in which she played Fred MacMurray's old-maid aunt. When MacMurray brings Barbara Stanwyck home for Christmas, Stanwyck is startled to find an old, never-used wedding dress in Patterson's trunk. "Was that yours?" Stanwyck asks softly. "Oh, I twiddled around with the idea one summer," Patterson says, making light of her long-ago heartbreak. "I was right again by fall."

"Boy, you're really a buff!" Lucy exclaimed when I finished the story. "You should meet my friend Robert Osborne. He knows the old ones just like you do."

For show business fans, the street where Lucy lived was famous. At one time or another Jack Benny, Oscar Levant, Agnes Moorehead, Ira Gershwin, Peter Falk, and Rosemary Clooney all lived on Roxbury. The same block. In 1985 James Stewart and his wife Gloria were still across the street. I don't remember how it came up, but Lucy started grumbling about a spate of neighborhood burglaries. "Jimmy and Gloria are worried," she said. "*We're* worried! Oh, it's awful. But I don't trust the Beverly Hills police as far as I can spit!"

The chaperone's slightly palsied hand reached out pleadingly and tapped me on the arm. "You're not going to put that in the story, are you?"

Same thing a few minutes later when I asked Lucy about her

son Desi Jr., a recovering alcoholic, and the inspirational lectures he delivered on sobriety. "Yeah, he's still doing that," Lucy groaned. "But at least he's not so *boring* about it now." The hand tapped my arm and the minder whispered, "You won't use that, will you?"

And a third time. While filming *Stone Pillow* in New York City, Lucy confided, she was so weak from the long hours and from wearing a heavy costume in oppressive heat that she contracted amoebic dysentery. She flew home, dehydrated and twenty-three pounds lighter, and fell into the gutter while entering a limo at LAX: "I was really *sick*!" she exclaimed with big eyes and that froggy, bottom-of-the-well voice. Once again the weathered hand reached out to me: "Please don't mention amoebic dysentery in your story," he implored.

I asked Lucy to grade herself, A to F, in several categories. She was game.

Mother? "B minus. I was deterred in many a way by working; I couldn't complete the scene at home."

Comedian? "Should I say A?"

"Yes!" I said.

"I guess I can because of the *I Love Lucy* reruns and the longevity still proving itself."

Dramatic actress? "I don't know, especially when my idol is Bette Davis. I haven't given it that much of a whack."

Business executive? "F. I hated it and I depended solely on honest and loyal men."

Late in the interview I asked Lucy for her zip code, so I could send her the article I was about to write. "I don't know my zip code," she declared in all earnestness. "I never write myself."

Moments later Lucy's husband walked in, looking very tan, well-kept and Beverly Hills-y in an alpaca cardigan and slacks.

"Gary, say hello to *old* Ed Guthmann!" Lucy croaked. Gary grinned, took my camera, and shot the photo you see here.

She was terrific. I'm sorry it was the only time I got to spend with her. If only, I thought later, I'd asked her to teach me back-gammon and if only Lucy had managed to ditch the geriatric minder and offer me a cocktail. We could've had a great time.

Chapter Twenty
Gregory Peck:
A Man Who Lived Up to The Myth

Two people, a father and a son, spend the night side by side. The sleeping child, Jem, has broken his arm in a spooky accident. The father, seated in a chair, is Atticus Finch, a wise attorney who knows instinctively that if Jem ever needed his loving presence, this is the time.

"He would be there all night," Jem's sister, Scout, observes in the lovely narration to *To Kill a Mockingbird*, "and he would be there when Jem waked up in the morning."

With those simple words, written in 1960 and repeated in the landmark 1962 film, *Mockingbird* author Harper Lee captured the beauty, gravity and fragility of parent-child relationships.

One couldn't separate Peck, who died June 12, 2003, at eighty-seven, from his greatest role. Just as the actor breathed life into the character, so the character illuminated and perhaps expanded the actor's warmth and humanity. The two were completely fused.

I found this true in 1989, when I flew to Los Angeles for an interview with Peck. The occasion was a press junket for *Old Gringo*, a movie that few remember and that meant little to me at the time. I was meeting my childhood hero. I was meeting Atticus Finch.

As a seventh-grader, I read Lee's novel and loved it. It was

With Gregory Peck.

the first "grown-up book" I'd read, and it opened the door to a world of conflicts and moral lessons I hadn't considered. Racial equality, respect for community, commitment to social justice —all that, plus the love of a widowed man for his two children.

When I saw the movie soon afterward, the beauty of *Mockingbird* was burned into my brain and my heart—so much so that I can't imagine what my childhood might have been without the book and film as touchstones.

I didn't realize it or articulate it this way at the time, but Atticus Finch was the father I wished I had had. Like many boys and girls, I had a troubled relationship with my father. Unlike Atticus, my dad had a quick temper and a harsh tongue. Unlike Atticus, he didn't have time for intimate talks, didn't become my navigator through the mysteries and passages of childhood.

Twenty-seven years after opening the book and seeing the film, I walked into a hotel room in Westwood and shook hands with Gregory Peck. He was tall, impressively so, dressed in a seersucker suit and matching necktie, his gray hair falling slightly onto his forehead. He spoke in that familiar, deep, and comforting voice.

From the moment we sat down, he exuded all the grace and kindness I'd associated with him. I've done hundreds of interviews with actors and film personalities, but few compare to Peck. He was everything I hoped he would be and more.

I started the interview telling him how I had rented a video of *Mockingbird* and watched it through a lot of tears, especially when Scout says, "He would be there when Jem waked up in the morning."

Peck wasn't bored by having to speak about his signature role one more time; he didn't steer the conversation away from *Mockingbird* in order to push the *Old Gringo* agenda. I think he recognized instantly how important it was to me and decided to give me, as he must have to countless others, the satisfaction of telling him what *To Kill a Mockingbird* meant to me.

"It has that effect on people," he said. "You know, they're still running it for seventh- and eighth-graders. I get letters from teachers all over the country, and sometimes they send a stack of essays the students have written, telling what the book and movie meant to them."

A lot of the kids, he said, mention the moment when racist Bob Ewell spits in Atticus's face because he defended the black man accused of raping Ewell's daughter. "Some of the boys say, 'Mr. Peck, you should've clobbered him.' And others will say, 'You were right, you lived up to your own teachings.' "

The other recurrent theme in those letters, Peck said, was

"the relationship between the father and the children. A lot of them sound a little bit forlorn in that they don't have that kind of relationship with their father."

He answered my questions about Mary Badham, the young actress who had played Scout, reporting that she'd settled in Virginia, married a schoolteacher, and worked in a ladies' dress shop. Philip Alford, who played Jem, was still in Alabama. "Of all things," Peck said, "he's making documentaries and commercials in Birmingham."

We talked about Harper Lee and why she'd never written another book. (Her novel *Go Set a Watchman* was posthumously published in 2015.) When *Mockingbird* was being shot on a back lot at Universal Studios, Peck said, all the actors were caught up in the emotion of the story. "The trick was to keep your emotions under control and not let them spill over."

When the interview was finished, I asked my favorite actor if he would pose for a picture with me. He said yes and stood next to me—just as Atticus Finch, the ideal dad, would do. That photo gives me a terrific feeling of warmth and peacefulness. How odd that Hollywood, a breeding ground for swollen egos, should produce a figure so temperate, so generous and inspiring as Gregory Peck.

Is it stretching things to say he was put on earth to show us how to be better people, better parents? It's hard for me to believe otherwise.

Chapter Twenty-one

Confessions of a
Recovering Movie Critic

I never asked to be a movie critic. People don't believe me when I say this. They assume movie reviewing is such a plum job that I must have scrambled and hustled for it. But that's not my story.

In 1991 I'd been at the *San Francisco Chronicle* seven years when the senior movie critic Judy Stone retired. In a crisp email, the assistant managing editor informed me that henceforth I would report full-time as a movie critic. There wasn't any "Come to my office to discuss..." conversation. No "How would you feel about...?"

I was the logical choice, I guess. I'd been pinch-hitting for Judy and two other critics when they got sick or went on vacation. Also, I'd previously reviewed movies for the *San Francisco Bay Guardian*, an alternative weekly. That job came unbidden, too: my next-door neighbor in Oakland was the *Guardian*'s arts editor and he had a hunch I could do it.

Despite my lifelong passion for movies and movie history, I never yearned to be a critic. I figured my take on movies was too idiosyncratic, too personal and off-the-mainstream. Eventually, I realized that *every* film critic is idiosyncratic— that taste and aesthetics by definition are deeply subjective. If a critic writes safe, generalized pabulum that doesn't spring from a strong point of view, and endeavors not to offend, nobody benefits and the readers don't learn a thing.

For the next twelve years I reviewed movies full-time in addition to writing profiles of movie personalities and occasional pieces on the business side of Hollywood. I saw between 200 and 250 movies per year and wrote up to five or six reviews and feature stories each week. I went to film festivals in Toronto, Berlin, Sundance, Telluride and Hong Kong. I got to champion international artists like Satyajit Ray (*The Apu Trilogy*) and Krzysztof Kieślowski (*The Double Life of Veronique*), whose films might otherwise have gone unnoticed because their distributors had such tiny advertising budgets. I was one of the first journalists to write about Oscar winners Alexander Payne (*The Holdovers*), Sofia Coppola (*Lost in Translation*) and Steven Soderbergh (*Erin Brockovich*) when their directing careers were just starting.

I saw movies in one of three ways: at a private, fifty-seat screening room in downtown San Francisco; at home with a cassette or DVD; or in a movie house packed with fans. Movie publicists prefer the latter because they want critics to see movies, particularly comedies, thrillers and musicals, with a large audience. That way, they figure, the critics absorb a contact high and review the film more favorably. So they rent a big theater and fill the seats by announcing ticket giveaways on a local radio station.

Praising a good movie, especially a little-known gem that would disappear without strong reviews, was gratifying. Reviewing bad movies was not. Too often, they were bad in the same way that bad movies were the week before. By granting them the attention of a review, I sometimes felt like I was justifying junk. The temptation was great to slam the stinkers and make them the butt of a wickedly phrased barb. That can be fun, but a critic shouldn't torch and pillage too often—not if you're basically entertaining yourself.

For each review, I assigned a Little Man. That's the rating system—one of five illustrations showing a tiny bald man in a chair—that the *Chronicle* uses instead of a four-star rating scale. Number one Little Man jumps out of his chair and applauds vigorously. Number two sits upright and applauds respectfully. Number three is alert but doesn't applaud. Number four is asleep. And number five is absent; his chair is empty.

I wasn't wild about the Little Man because he oversimplifies and literalizes an assessment. There's been talk at various times of retiring him, but readers love him, especially lifelong *Chronicle* readers. They feel a sentimental attachment. Occasionally, when I was still reviewing movies, a friend or colleague would introduce me by saying, "Hey, do you know who this is? This is 'The Little Man'!"

Being a movie critic brought me a minor level of renown and a taste of the privileges and annoyances of being a public person. I was always gratified when someone said, "You're my favorite critic" or "I saw that movie you recommended and loved it." It was fun seeing my name quoted in a newspaper ad or a movie trailer, or hearing from a cousin in Ohio when their local newspaper reprinted one of my reviews. I loved the dialogue with

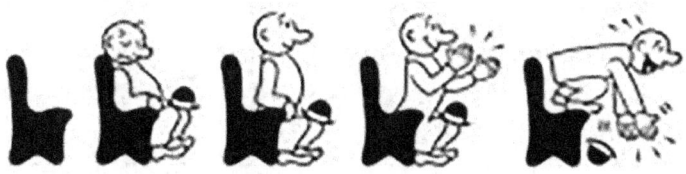

The Little Man, the *San Francisco Chronicle*'s movie-rating graphic.

readers and fringe benefits like getting choice seats and not waiting in long lines; getting comped for concerts and plays; having my phone calls answered quickly. A person gets spoiled that way, and I definitely was. My head swelled. Alarming how fast that will happen.

The notoriety wasn't always fun. When email replaced letter-writing as the standard communication mode in the early 1990s, feedback from readers quadrupled. Some correspondents were kind and thoughtful; many were not. I learned that anger, not satisfaction, is the great motivator when contacting a total stranger. Think about it: how often do you write your utility company and enthuse, "The heat in my apartment feels great on this blustery day. You guys are the best!"?

One day a fellow reviewer at the *Chronicle* asked me, "Are you getting a lot more hate mail?" I was. "You owe me the $10 I wasted on that piece of crap!" was a grumble I received more than once. Or, "Are you *sure* you saw the same movie I saw?" Or this classic: "It is clear in the last analysis that the only thing coursing through the mind and pen of Edward Guthmann is viciousness of the lowest sort." People take movies personally, and if you knock something that touches them or reinforces their belief system, they feel as if you've violated their essential being.

Once your name is public, you're fair game: Occasionally I got nasty phone messages at home—always anonymous. At a preview screening, I was photographed kamikaze-style from three feet away by the editor of a San Francisco literary journal. "You might ask first before you photograph someone," I said. "Ohhh, would the *Chronicle*?" he snarled. The next day he posted the photo online and claimed I "lashed out" at him.

In October 2003 I wrote my last review. Suddenly my weeknights were free. In that first year after I quit reviewing, I went to one or two movies a month instead of four or five a week. I saw what I wanted to see, and if I was bored I stood up and walked out—never an option when you're a critic. I felt liberated.

At the same time, I was giving up my cachet. I knew I would miss the communication with readers and the cushy, glamorous aspects of the job—like traveling to film festivals and meeting movie personalities. Being a critic gave me greater visibility and a wider readership than I'd ever known. But it wasn't my favorite gig and I don't regret stepping away.

The work that compels me most is writing profiles: the opportunity to shine a light and explore another person's life. When I burned out as a critic I pivoted to profiling authors, artists, diamonds in the rough. A man who survived a lobotomy at age twelve; an artist afflicted with acute photosensitivity who can't go outdoors; an eighty-seven-year-old grandmother whose gorgeous memoir of her Iowa childhood, *Little Heathens*, became a surprise bestseller. I loved getting off the movie beat and writing those pieces. It was the kind of journalism I'd wanted to do all along.

When Thom Gunn, a San Francisco poet, died, I constructed a two-part oral biography that interwove quotes from Gunn's friends and colleagues with fragments from Gunn's poems that amplified those quotes. Much earlier, in 1986, I wrote a large collection of stories and profiles illustrating the impact of AIDS on San Francisco's arts communities. Those two projects were my best work at the *Chronicle*.

In 2009 I started writing "What I Do," a weekly series spotlighting working folks describing their jobs. The Laotian immigrant shining shoes at Nordstrom; the eighty-four-year-old widow riding the streetcar each day to her job at an office supplies shop; the safecracker and the San Francisco Opera prompter; the Salvadoran lady barber and the rock 'n' roll drummer-turned-carpet-cleaner. Unlike Hollywood celebrities, the working people I profiled were unguarded, unmanaged, and grateful to tell their story to someone who wanted to listen.

It's that connection—the engagement with people I would never meet otherwise, the opportunity to "part a curtain" and tell their story—that never grows old.

Chapter Twenty-two
Willa, Eudora, Carson, & Others

In all the reading I've done in my life, the authors I return to most often are female. I think it's because women in their writing are attuned to the details and textures of life, to our inner lives.

Women have long been outsiders, relegated to the role of nurturer and helpmate, denied opportunities to develop autonomous lives. Outsiders are observers, equipped to see the world from a wider, nuanced perspective. From that flows the art.

There are three female authors in particular whose books I've read for decades and return to periodically, as if to an old friend.

My favorite, Willa Cather, is remarkable for her empathy—the warm, overseeing regard she has for her characters. Whereas much of today's fiction has the bite of cool, ironic detachment or outright cynicism, those qualities are absent in Cather's work. She's not mushy or sentimental, and she never spares her characters the harsh turns and disappointments of life. Rather, she observes their struggles with insight and an open heart, as if she were taking these people by the hand and gently presenting them, every aspect of them, to the reader.

She has abundant gifts but Cather's greatest, I think, is her ability to describe the landscape of the American Midwest and the Nebraska prairie: "I can remember exactly how the country looked to me as I walked beside my grandmother," the narrator says in *My Ántonia*, her most celebrated novel. "I felt motion in the landscape; in the fresh, easy-blowing morning wind, and in the earth itself, as if the shaggy grass were a loose hide, and underneath it herds of wild buffalo were galloping, galloping..."

Cather had an affinity for artists and loners, for young people starting out in life and the diminished elderly looking back with regret. Her heartbreaking short story "Paul's Case," about a stagestruck youth who leaves home with stolen money and briefly lives like a king, ends with one of the most devastating closing paragraphs in fiction. In one of her greatest novels, *Death Comes for the Archbishop*, she portrays the life of a French vicar establishing a Catholic church in 19th-century New Mexico. There's tenderness and understanding, a remarkably nonjudgmental view of cultural differences and displacement.

Cather was herself an outsider. In an era when being a lesbian demanded secrecy and subterfuge, she shared the last thirty-nine years of her life with magazine editor Edith Lewis. The nature of their relationship was never made public, and Cather arranged before her death in 1947 to have most of their correspondence destroyed.

Willa Cather

Another outsider, Carson McCullers, was as wickedly perverse as Cather was measured and kind. I just revisit-

Carson McCullers

ed McCullers's novella *The Ballad of the Sad Café* and found it even sadder and more powerful than when I read it in my thirties. It's only seventy pages, but it has gravity and depth, the rich atmosphere and foreboding of an ancient Gothic fable. It's the story of Amelia, mannish and six-feet-two, who runs a general store and makes moonshine in her dreary Georgia town. Friend to none, she astounds the townspeople by taking a lover named Cousin Lymon, a gregarious dwarf hunchback.

In *Ballad*, McCullers has a stunning passage about "the lover and the beloved" that encapsulates the overriding theme of her work. "A most mediocre person can be the object of a love which is wild, extravagant, and beautiful as the poison lilies of the swamp," she writes. "A good man may be the stimulus for a love both violent and debased, or a jabbering madman may bring about in the soul of someone a tender and simple idyll."

McCullers wrote about the lonely and outcast—people who, like tomboy Frankie Addams in *The Member of the Wedding*, yearn to experience "the we of me." There's a scampish wit in many of her stories and a wonderful facility for dialogue. Take Berenice Sadie Brown, Frankie's plain-speaking nanny and housekeeper: Ask her opinion and she will give you an answer, blunt and unvarnished. When Frankie wonders why Berenice doesn't marry Mr. T.T. Williams, the very proper Black gentleman who regularly takes her out to dinner, Berenice says, "I respect him and regard him highly. But he don't make me shiver none."

McCullers, raised in Georgia, was twice married and divorced from Reeves McCullers, an alcoholic who committed suicide at forty. She did her best writing in her twenties, suffered a series of strokes and died at fifty, in 1967. "Of all the Southern writers," Gore Vidal wrote, "she is the most apt to endure."

Eudora Welty, another Southern writer, lacked the darker bent of McCullers, but shared her appreciation for eccentricity and her ear for colloquial speech. Welty had a delicious, subtle humor and sometimes drew story ideas from gossip overheard at the Jitney Jungle grocery store in Jackson, Mississippi, where she lived for nearly all her ninety-two years.

She wrote five novels, including the Pulitzer Prize winner *The Optimist's Daughter,* but the short story was her true métier. *A Curtain of Green*, her first published collection, was my introduction to Welty, and I suggest it as a starting point. It includes the celebrated masterpiece "Why I Live at the P.O.," as well as "Old Mr. Marblehall" (his wife "spent her life trying to escape from the parlor-like jaws of self-consciousness") and "A Worn Path," about an old Black woman trekking through deep piney woods to buy medicine for her grandson.

Welty once wrote that her guiding impetus in storytelling was "not to point the finger of judgment, but to part a curtain, that

Eudora Welty

invisible shadow that falls between people." She had the ability to enter her characters' minds and capture their voices, their joys and delusions.

In 2009, eight years after her death, I traveled to Jackson to get a sense of her world and write about it for the *San Francisco Chronicle*. The main branch of the Jackson public library was named for her, the local theater had a playwriting competition in her name, and a bust of her head greeted the visitor on entering the town's premier independent bookshop.

I visited the Eudora Welty House at 1119 Pinehurst Street, where she resided, with few exceptions, ever since her family moved there in 1925. Comfortable and unpretentious, the Tudor Revival home had become a National Historic Landmark managed by Welty's niece Mary Alice White.

Instead of a museum layout with glass-enclosed photographs and educational displays, the Welty House landmark replicates how the home looked in the 1980s. One gets the feeling that the occupant—tall, graceful, with a voice like honeyed bourbon—

Eudora Welty's house in Jackson, Mississippi.

had just stepped out to run errands. In the living room is the floral-print armchair where Welty sat each day, next to a TV tray holding a letter opener, stamps, paper clips, coasters, and a box of Aunt Sally's Pralines from New Orleans.

Books are everywhere. They've covered the coffee table, colonized the dining table, laid claim to the Steinway piano that Welty's mother bought in the 1920s by selling quart bottles of milk from a cow at the family's previous home. Next to the kitchen and breakfast room is the "hospitality area" where Welty mixed cocktails for her best pals every Thursday night, a bottle of her beloved Maker's Mark bourbon given pride of place on the counter.

Welty never married, although she maintained an avid correspondence and romance of sorts, probably unconsummated, with detective writer Ross Macdonald. "As you have seen, I am a writer who came of a sheltered life," she told a Harvard University audience in 1983. "A sheltered life can be a daring life as well. For all serious daring starts from within."

Chapter Twenty-three
Libraries: A Love Story

When I was growing up, the public library would send a woman to ring your doorbell if you were delinquent in returning overdue books. She was perky and neighborly and had a kind smile. I remember my mom searching for a book, which she'd uncharacteristically forgotten about, and apologizing as she handed it over to the volunteer.

I can't imagine that happening today, what with libraries suffering budget cuts and people afraid to open their doors to strangers. But I'm glad I grew up in a time when that practice existed, because it reinforced for me the sense that libraries are special places built on democratizing principles; that reading is salvation and a gift; that library books are public property and not meant to be hoarded.

In my hometown of West Covina there was a little library in a storefront across from the Presbyterian church. I remember the slightly musty smell, the hushed and polite ambience, the peaceful, engaged faces of the patrons. I could sit down right now and draw you a floor map of all the bookcases, the tables, and the circulation desk. I remember checking out Harriet Beecher Stowe's Civil War classic *Uncle Tom's Cabin* when I was eight or nine, much to the librarian's astonishment ("How old are you?" she asked), and then not being able to read it because the language was so outdated.

The original, very modest West Covina Public Library. Where my love of books began.

When I was ten or eleven, the city built a new, much-larger library near the city hall and police station. This was a big civic event. There must have been five times as many books at the new facility. I discovered the periodicals section where newspapers were draped on slotted poles and arranged horizontally in racks. I would pull the Sunday *New York Times* and feast on the Arts & Leisure section with its news of Broadway shows and foreign films—a cherished window into a world of sophistication that from West Covina seemed remote. They even had a large record section, where I discovered Bizet's *Carmen* sung by Leontyne Price—my introduction to opera.

One day, I think I was twelve, I found a book on the making of *The Misfits,* the last movie for both Marilyn Monroe and Clark Gable. The clerk at the counter was a clenched scold and she refused to check the book out to me. I found my mother in another part of the library and without missing a beat she walked me back to the counter and asked the clerk to explain herself. "Well, it's *The Misfits!*" the woman said as if the title alone could lead a young reader to filth and degradation. "He's not old enough for that."

"My son reads at an adult level," my mother said, "and you have no right to refuse to check out this or any other book to him." She was indignant and fired-up that afternoon, qualities she rarely evinced. I remember the surprise and the charge I felt as she brilliantly defended my civil rights and put the moralizing prude in her place. My mother prevailed and I took that book home. I found nothing even slightly lurid in it, just gossip about Marilyn's personal demons and on-set tardiness.

Going to the library was always an occasion, something my mom, my younger brother Dave and I seemed to enjoy equally. Since our suburban town was spread out and lacked public transportation, I was dependent on my mother to drive me. I often checked out multiple books and ended up not reading many of them. I read my first adult book, *To Kill a Mockingbird,* in seventh grade; fell in love with Pearl S. Buck's *The Good Earth* in tenth grade; and was dazzled by early installments of Truman Capote's *In Cold Blood* in *The New Yorker*—read aloud by my high school journalism teacher Martha Lupton Schneidewind.

In college, I scored a job at the campus library and worked at the circulation desk. A dream job. I loved getting a behind-the-scenes view of library operations, the voyeuristic pleasure of seeing which books and magazines various people checked out. When I took a Shakespeare class I discovered the library's large collection of plays on vinyl. You could rent a headset, schedule time at a turntable and hear Laurence Olivier and Maggie Smith performing *Othello* or Richard Burton's anguished *Hamlet.* With money earned working at that library, I financed a summer-long trip to Europe.

My relationship with libraries is deep and affectionate, and I feel a strong sense of offended justice when I see library books defaced, mistreated or stolen. In college I went to the home of

Library of Congress, Washington, D.C. The granddaddy of United States libraries. *Photo by Steve Schmid.*

a spacey hippie I knew and commented on a handsome art book that was overdue from the campus library. "Oh yeah," she said with an airy shrug. "I liked it so much I decided to keep it.'" I should have rescued that book and returned it to its rightful place.

Today, I use my neighborhood library constantly. I read three or four books a month, most of them library books. I check out music and movies on DVD and frequently go to oaklandlibrary.org to place a hold, schedule a renewal, or just peruse titles by certain authors (lately I'm obsessed with Steinbeck). I have my gripes: Libraries aren't nearly as quiet as they were when I was a kid and often become unofficial day care centers for the stroller brigade of nannies and toddlers. There's a lack of professional comportment among staff, too: you see employees looking like they came off the soccer field in T-shirts and jeans. Once I saw the neighborhood branch manager wearing his shirttail out. Yep, I'm old-school: I respect libraries and I think the people who operate them should dress like they do, too.

Last year I read Susan Orlean's *The Library Book,* a wonderful study of the Los Angeles Public Library's downtown facility:

how in 1986 it suffered a massive seven-hour fire that destroyed over a million books; how it recovered and today serves an amazingly wide demographic, including a large homeless population; how it adapts to changing times and continues to redefine the social, educational, and spiritual functions of a public library.

Like me, Orlean formed her connection to libraries early in life, starting from regular visits with her mother. I've always admired her writing, and *The Library Book* is one book I wish I had written myself. It captures beautifully the magic of libraries and the gratitude that devotees like myself feel all our lives.

With the amazing Lucy.

Chapter Twenty-four
I Like Dogs

Every time I see a dog in a movie or a TV commercial, my focus drifts to the dog and the people on screen disappear. If I see a dog on the street, in a park or especially on a beach where they romp through the water, I instantly feel better. Dogs are thrilled to be outdoors with the abundant smells, fresh air and stimuli. Their gait quickens, their mouths open in a happy grin. Exhilaration flows pure and unchecked.

Human-dog contact is a win-win. We draw a sense of stillness and comfort from stroking a dog's coat, and they in turn luxuriate in the touch of our hands. Dogs love the smooth softness of human fingers and palms, the way our individually articulated digits work in concert to scratch or massage them. They don't get that from other animals.

"Even just watching an animal can take you out of your mind," wrote German author Eckhart Tolle. "[The animal] is more deeply connected with the source of life than most humans, and that rootedness in Being transmits itself to you. Millions of people who otherwise would be completely lost in the conceptual reality of their mind are kept sane by living with an animal."

I love the honesty of dogs, their devotion and exuberance. I love their goofiness, their unembarrassed displays of affection.

Their inherent goodness. I'm undone when I hear about neglected or abused dogs or any form of animal cruelty. Twice I've tried to read Jack London's *The Call of the Wild* and both times had to put the book down when Buck, a 140-pound Saint Bernard–Scotch Shepherd mix, is kidnapped, sold to a dog trader, and savagely beaten with a club.

I love dogs for their vulnerability and resilience. They live in our world with its risks and hazards—cars, trucks, human neglect and mistreatment—and yet they're always eager to re-engage with us. I love their intuition: when dogs encounter a newborn baby, for example, they know instinctively this life is new and fragile and they approach tenderly.

There are two things I don't like about dogs: 1) they die way too soon; and 2) they can't tell you when they're sick and where they hurt. Canine stoicism can mask a lot of discomfort, when all you want is to make them feel better.

Today I live with Lucy, a fourteen-year-old Labrador Retriever. She's just about perfect. Funny, gentle and soulful, friendly with everyone. If anger and aggression were measured on a scale of one to one hundred, one hundred being the worst, Lucy would be a solid zero. She came that way, so I can't claim credit. I just feel very, very lucky.

———•———

When I was five or six, my parents brought home a black-and-white puppy. We named him Smitty, after an old newspaper comic strip. He was beautiful—I still remember his sweet smell —but my brothers and I were too young to know how to handle a puppy and my parents weren't much help, either. Neither had ever owned a dog. Dad didn't want Smitty in the house at night because he wasn't potty-trained, and instead of putting him in

Smitty and my brother Davey, 1956.

the backyard with a little dog house, he stuck him in the garage and shut the door. It was windowless and unheated, and when I opened the garage door in the morning I'd find a frightened, yelping Smitty, piles of poop and a rank stench.

Smitty didn't last long. My brother Danny and I teased him, or so I remember my parents saying, and when he bit a little girl across the street my dad took Smitty away for good. I don't know if he was put down or given a new home. That was never revealed.

———•———

Five years passed and one day Dad brought home a large, snow-white dog named Nitre ("Nee-trah"). She was completely un-interested in our family, numb to encouragement or affection, and soon we discovered why. The family that gave her up had a horse to which she was deeply bonded. A few days after we

Nitre

acquired her, Nitre ran away and miraculously found her way to her former home and equine companion, two or three miles away. We brought her back to our house, and the next day she escaped again. Did the previous owners change their mind and keep Nitre, or was she taken to the pound? I don't remember.

———— ♦ ————

We didn't stop trying. When I was twelve, the *San Gabriel Valley Tribune* announced that kids under ten could run a free classified ad during Easter Week. Davey, then eight, submitted the ad copy: "Family of five looking for a dog. Must be house-trained." Lots of calls came in; we looked at several dogs and chose Rusty, a three-year-old cocker spaniel whose owner was allergic to dog fur.

Rusty was cute—a docked tail, big brown eyes, and gorgeous reddish-brown coat—but he was a total nut and not too smart. You couldn't walk him because he pulled so wildly on the leash and couldn't be trained not to. He hated other dogs, and when we took him to a school playground for a rabies shot, Rusty barked so uncontrollably at the other dogs that he threw up and had to be taken home. At Balboa Beach the next year, he reacted so angrily to the waves breaking on the shoreline that he refused to go near the water. Hopeless.

Rusty's major talent unfolded every weekday when we watched *Jeopardy!*, a mainstay in our house. He was captivated by the Final Jeopardy theme music ("Doo-doo-doo, Dah-dah, Doo-DOO-doo"), and during those thirty seconds he would arch his neck and howl like a wolf serenading the moon. If a friend came over, we'd turn up the volume to maximize Rusty's entertainment value. He always delivered.

I cringe remembering this, but my brothers and I were sometimes awful to Rusty. We thought it was fun to turn on the garden hose, get him soaking wet and laugh as he barked in anger. No surprise, then, that he learned to equate us with trouble. He favored my father, which was odd since my brothers and I

Rusty with Dad on his Archie Bunker recliner, 1965.

were so frequently at odds with Dad. Every day at 5:30 p.m., Rusty would lie in front of the door, his nose pointed faithfully in anticipation. Then wag, wag, wag when Dad walked in. After dinner Dad sat in his Archie Bunker recliner and slapped his knee. Rusty jumped on the chair, rolled on his back and purred as Dad massaged his tummy, saying "Such a good boy, isn't he? *Such* a good boy."

———◆———

I didn't see much of Rusty after I left for college, and when I was living in the Bay Area and working full-time I didn't get a dog because I wasn't home enough. Finally, in my forties I brought home Nicky, a thirteen-year-old cocker spaniel with big floppy ears and an angelic disposition. Nicky had a good life with a married couple I knew, but when they adopted a little girl and Nicky snapped at her they looked for a new home.

Nicky was the same breed as Rusty, but they couldn't have been more different. He rarely barked and seemed to like and trust everyone. Two months after I adopted him, as we were walking across a parking lot entrance, Nicky was hit by a car.

Emergency surgery for internal bleeding and an abdominal hernia seemed to work, but two weeks later Nicky couldn't stand up or walk. An embolism had formed in the blood vessel connecting to his spinal cord, paralyzing his back legs.

"I think you should put him down," a young vet ad-

Nicky, an angel.

vised. But I knew Nicky had more life in him, so I ordered a custom-made, two-wheeled doggie wheelchair. It was tough at first: I'd slip Nicky into the harness and strap his back legs to the stirrups that elevated his posterior. He was initially confused but soon learned to power himself through the house and the neighborhood with his front legs. He learned to go in reverse, turn corners and chase squirrels. Nicky never felt sorry for himself.

Helping Nicky adjust to his new life was a lesson in love. He inspired me with his dignity and perseverance—his lovely, unvanquished spirit. People often remarked on his chariot. "What happened to your dog?" they'd ask, followed by "Is that permanent?" and "Did you make that yourself?" It drove me batty if someone said. "Oh, poor thing..." because he was so clearly a hero. Nicky died two years later, at fifteen, and I don't think I ever cried as much. It's amazing how deeply a dog's love can burrow into your heart.

———————◆———————

A year later I heard about another cocker spaniel at the SPCA. Freddie was a three-year-old who'd already been adopted twice and surrendered twice. I should've taken that as a warning because, even though he was cute and amusing, Freddie was a strange and difficult dog. He wasn't exactly companionable, and he tended to destroy anything at his level—a pair of leather gloves, eyeglass frames, soiled tissues

Freddie, wearing a lei.

from the wastebasket. He was expensive, too. When he developed thrombocytopenia, which is the failure of bone marrow to produce sufficient blood platelets, he became anemic.

Freddie died in 2007 and I let four years pass before adopting a new dog. I contacted Canine Companions for Independence, an organization that breeds and trains service dogs. Sixty percent of their canine trainees don't complete the program, usually because of distractibility, at which point they go up for adoption. I was on a waiting list for a year before I got an email saying a beautiful, one-year-and-nine-month-old female was available. Three-quarters Labrador Retriever and one-quarter Golden Retriever. She'd been pulled from training because she was afraid of stairs. When I met her on the CCI campus in Santa Rosa one afternoon, it was very easy to say, *Yes, absolutely. I'll take her.*

Lucy is my miracle—one of the best things that ever happened to me. From the get-go she was sweet, quiet, undemanding, and adorable. So chill and serene that, even at two years old, people mistook her for an older dog, She's beautiful in a purely aesthetic sense, with deep brown eyes, short blond eyelashes, and a wavy yellow coat, and she's elegant in her disposition. I love the purring sound she makes when snoring. She's a "talker" in general, expressing herself with little grumbles, rumbles, murmurs, and snorts.

When Lucy was young she was nuts for the ball. She'd play for an hour, racing to the ball and trotting back with her tail standing straight-up to say, "Look what I did!" Being a Lab, she loves water. She learned to swim at a dog-friendly beach on San Francisco Bay, but her true place of enchantment is Limantour Beach at Point Reyes National Seashore. The beach stretches four miles along Drakes Bay and when the fog lifts you can see the San Francisco skyline to the south. The sand is soft, the tall

Lucy at her happy place, Limantour Beach.

Ammophila beach grasses separate the beach from the dunes, and the surf is often gentle. Perfect for a dog to chase a ball and circle back through the receding tide to cool off.

As I write this, Lucy is an old lady of fourteen. Creaky joints, diminished hearing, very slow on walks. She sleeps fourteen to sixteen hours a day, doesn't run any more, but still loves to eat. Loves to walk the neighborhood and sniff its olfactory smorgasbord. Loves to greet random strangers. Lucy's gotten bold in her dotage: she approaches people she doesn't know, requiring no encouragement on their part. Simply lifts her face, shows her deep brown eyes and brushes her soft furry muzzle against their leg, asking for affection and a possible treat.

"Be my friend, OK?"

On a German freight steamer bound for Cameroun, 1928. Front: Roberta, Winifred, Esther. Back row at left: my grandmother Roberta Brown Hope.

Chapter Twenty-five
The Hope Sisters

The waitress smiled when I told her I'd just flown in from California. "So what brings you to Chicago?" she asked.

"This is going to sound really strange," I said, "but I came here for a gorilla."

She looked puzzled. "My aunt and cousin are driving up from Cincinnati and we're going to visit him at the Field Museum. My aunt knew him a long time ago in Africa."

True story. Bushman was a western lowland gorilla and when he was separated from his mother in the early 1930s, a big-game trader left him with my missionary grandparents in Cameroun. He was still a baby—an adorable baby—and during that year became the beloved pet of my mother and her sisters.

After a year the trader, Julius Buck, took Bushman to the States and sold him to the Lincoln Park Zoo in Chicago. He grew to be the largest ape in captivity—550 pounds—and became the zoo's star attraction.

When Bushman was ailing and thought to be dying, an estimated 120,000 people lined up to see him in a single day. After his death in 1951 he was preserved at the Field Museum of Natural History, also in Chicago, where he remains on display today.

I explained this to the waitress that evening in 2013, adding

Bushman at Lincoln Park Zoo, soon after he arrived in Chicago, 1931.

During his 20 years at the zoo, Bushman was a star attraction.

that the following day I would meet my Aunt Winifred, who was ninety-two, for her reunion with Bushman.

———◆———

As a kid, I figured out early that my family story was unusual. It probably started when I saw photos of my mother at age eleven holding a baby gorilla. My curiosity about her early life never faded, and in 1993 I finished *Return to Cameroun,* a one-hour documentary about my missionary grandparents and their lives in Africa. At the heart of the movie are interviews I filmed at a family reunion with my mother Roberta and my four aunts —Arta Grace, Betty, Esther, and Winifred—and footage from a trip I took to Cameroun with Esther and Winifred in 1989. Actors Gena Rowlands and Pat Hingle became the voices of my grandparents, reading selections from letters they wrote home from Africa.

I made the movie because I wanted to learn more about my grandparents Fred and Roberta Hope, both of whom died before I was born. In the process I also got to know my mom and aunts much better. They were lovely women, similar in their modesty and lack of pretense, but absolutely individual.

Arta Grace was the oldest, a voracious reader, so quiet you might never notice her sly and playful wit. She married a biology professor from the Smoky Mountains of Tennessee, had four children, and worked as a librarian. Shy and self-effacing, Arta Grace didn't smile or face the camera in most of the photographs I've seen of her.

Betty, a year younger, was also reticent, the opposite of her convivial, garrulous husband. She was the only Hope sister to become a missionary and she spent most of her working life in France, at a Bible institute north of Paris. I have a special feeling

The Hope sisters with their mother, 1922. Front row: Esther, Roberta, my grandmother holding Winifred. Back row: Betty and Arta Grace.

for Betty because she was meek and gentle and lacking in vanity. In her, those qualities felt like a kind of purity. When I visited her in Europe as a twenty-year-old, Aunt Betty's warmth and hospitality were so great that after saying goodbye and boarding a train I started to cry. She lived to be 100.

Esther was the middle child: a nurse, mother of six, and grandmother of twenty-three. She had a hearty laugh, big pink cheeks like you see in popular images of Mrs. Santa Claus, and a cheerful, radiant smile. "She is a regular piece of sunshine," my grandmother wrote when Esther was just one year old. "People almost have to get happy when she comes around." That never changed.

My mother, Roberta, was kind and modest, a great listener and obliging partner to my volatile father. She was the prettiest of the Hope sisters. Warm eyes, gorgeous smile. Like Esther, she worked as a nurse until she got married. I adored her and, although we got closer in her later years, there was a reserve in my mother, a resistance to disclosure or self-reflection that made her slightly unknowable. I still have a strong urge to see her. It feels like a conversation, sharply interrupted, that I'm waiting to resume.

Winifred, the youngest, was a talker and a storyteller, the steward of a vast repository of family memories. She was more attuned to popular culture than the average senior citizen—in her late sixties she described something that "really grossed me out"—but acutely sensitive and easily hurt. She married a quiet man who was her opposite, worked as a church secretary, and at one time started a biography of my grandfather Fred that she never finished.

I was raised in California and since my aunts lived far away —Betty in France, Arta Grace in Tennessee, Esther and Winifred in Cincinnati—I rarely saw them when I was growing up. As an adult I made a commitment to building friendships with each of them. I flew twice to Tennessee to visit Arta Grace, saw Esther and Winifred in Cincinnati, and on several trips to Europe made detours to visit Aunt Betty and Uncle Bob—first in France and later in Belfast, where they retired.

The more time I spent with them, the more I appreciated their resilience in surviving a childhood that, for all its exoticism and adventure, was marked by long separations and displacement. There were no schools for missionary kids above the sixth grade in Cameroun, so none of the Hope sisters stayed beyond the age of twelve or thirteen. They remained in the United States and only saw their parents during the one-year furloughs that separated three-year terms in the mission field.

When I was making *Return to Cameroun* and heard the Hope sisters describing their extraordinary childhood in Africa, I

At a family reunion in Cincinnati, 1985. Roberta, Arta Grace, Esther, Betty. Seated: Winifred and I.

remember thinking that at certain moments, as their faces brightened, they seemed to revert to the wide-eyed astonishment of childhood. It was wonderful to see that.

"I had oh, maybe twenty caterpillars that I had found," Arta Grace, seventy-six at the time, remembered. "They were green and they had gold spikes on

Arta Grace, Betty and a papaya tree. Cameroun, 1916.

them. They were beautiful and I had been keeping them in a shoebox all day and putting leaves in for them to eat." Later that afternoon, "I looked under the house and saw a young African boy eating them. He would look at me and chew and grin. Then drop another caterpillar in his mouth and chew some more.

"I didn't mind that he was eating caterpillars," she said with an almost-imperceptible impish smile. "What bothered me was that they were *my* caterpillars."

The Hope sisters talked about sailing to Africa on a German freight steamer that stopped at every West African port to load on goats, horses and pigs, huge bunches of bananas and other cargo with a large crane. They remembered eating Camerounian papayas ("paw-paws") as big as watermelons; driver ants that traveled en masse through their house and bit them in their sleep; and Minkie, a rascally monkey with amber eyes, a white nose and 27-inch-long tail, who went back to Indiana with the family and died of frostbite when he was left in the greenhouse one winter.

They talked about drawing sap from rubber trees and chewing it like gum; about the industrial school where my Grandfather Fred taught tailoring, carpentry, bricklaying, and other self-sustaining trades to the men of southern Cameroun. They remembered the drums made from hollowed-out logs that sent coded bulletins—like a telegraph—from village to village. "One drum would beat out the message," Winifred said, "and the drummer in the next village would repeat it, and that was how they sent a message from the coast to the interior."

They talked about their parents, who met in 1911 at a New York City conference for outgoing missionaries, got engaged days later on a ship bound for England, and were married on a German freight steamer en route to Cameroun. Fred Hope was a farm boy from southern Illinois, robust and shaped like a barrel, with a hearty laugh and big open heart. His father had fought in the Civil War and spent two years at Andersonville, an infamous Confederate prison-of-war camp. Fred was a man of integrity who, when a relative incurred a large gambling debt, chose to drop out of school and work the family farm until the debt was paid. He went back to high school in his early twenties, started college at twenty-five.

Roberta Brown, my grandmother, was a preacher's daughter and a schoolteacher, raised in Iowa and North Dakota. She was staid and formal, disinclined to demonstrations of affection. "I don't remember my mother ever putting her arms around me and kissing me and saying 'I love you,' " my mother said. "But I never had any doubt that she loved me." My grandmother had a gift for languages and art. She mastered both German and Bulu, the tribal language in Cameroun, and brought her delicate, skillful hand to family photographs that she retouched with watercolors.

And, of course, the Hope Sisters remembered Bushman, the baby gorilla who spent a year with the Hope family in Cameroun. "He was like a live doll to me," my mother said. "Like having a baby to take care of. [We] carried him around, fed him. Even put clothes on him, like kids will."

"Oh, Bushman was a dear soul," Winifred said. "He was a spoiled baby, is what he was. We carried him around everywhere and if you put him down he'd grab ahold of your leg and sit on your foot. And then you'd walk along with this big ape hangin' on your foot."

The sisters grew up speaking Bulu and English with equal fluency. Bulu was such a vital aspect of their childhood that when Arta Grace arrived in the United States for the first time at

Esther with unnamed baby gorilla, Winifred holding Minkie, my mother Roberta holding Bushman, 1930.

age three, she ran up to an African American woman she saw on the streets of New York. Throwing her arms around the woman's legs, Arta Grace wept and spoke to the startled lady in Bulu.

All five sisters felt the sting of being left behind in the States while their parents worked in Africa. Arta Grace and Betty spent six years—two missionary terms—with their blind grandmother and unmarried aunt in the small farming town of Flat Rock, Illinois. "I think they loved us but they didn't show it in any way," Betty wrote in an essay about her life. "I cried myself to sleep the first Christmas Eve."

Their Grandmother Hope was tough, self-reliant. During the Civil War Betsie was in her teens, and with the men fighting for the North she worked the farm herself. Tended crops and livestock, split logs to build fence posts. Sixty years later, with her granddaughters in her care, "Grandma was afraid something would happen to us," Betty said. "She didn't allow us to go anywhere—only to school and church and Sunday school." No friends. Those years "affected Arta Grace and me both," she added. "I always felt shy with strangers and I'm sure that's where it originated."

Esther had it the roughest. When she was six and her parents were ready to sail back to Cameroun, her maternal grandmother Grace Hill Brown insisted that my grandparents leave one of the girls with her. "She was really making a pest of herself, because she felt Mother and Dad were showing favorites by leaving Arta Grace and Betty with Grandma Hope," Esther said. "Finally, to shut her up, Dad said, 'All right, we'll call Esther in and see what she says. And what she says, that's what we'll do.' "

Esther didn't understand the question. She said yes. "I thought it was just a two-week lark or something like that," she remembered. Her father Fred was loath to renege on a prom-

The Hope family in Indiana, 1928, on furlough between missionary terms in Africa. Left to right: Esther, Roberta, Winifred, Arta Grace, Betty. My grandparents Fred and Roberta Brown Hope stand behind them.

ise, so he left Esther behind in Winona Lake, Indiana, for three years. No other children in the house. A horrible mistake. "He didn't dream I would choose to stay with Grandma," Esther said. "It was a blow that my dad never really did get over, and we were never as close again after that."

I'm sure the decision to divide the family wasn't callous or capricious on my grandparents' part. "I seriously considered giving up the work in the mission field because of them," my grandfather once wrote. "You do not know the heart longing and anxious hours and prayer that we've gone through while away from them." But I wonder—apart from feeling they were serving God—how they rationalized their decision.

In 1928, Esther returned to Cameroun with her parents and two younger sisters. Soon the Hope family was fostering baby

Bushman, as well as mischievous Minkie—but it was to be the Hope sisters' last time in Africa. In their teens they were sent to a boarding school for missionary children in Columbia, South Carolina, run by my grandfather's pious, starchy cousin Josephine Hope Westervelt. Her methods were antediluvian: Girls weren't allowed to talk to boys and ate separately from them.

When my grandparents returned to the U.S. after a three-year commitment in Africa, and convened with their daughters in Indiana, it took months for the Hopes to settle into a familial rhythm. "One thing that made me kind of suddenly shy," Esther remembered, "was when my mother came to get me and I looked out the window and said, '*Who is that?*'"

"I know a lot of missionary children feel cheated," my mother Roberta said in *Return to Cameroun*. "They feel that their parents didn't show real love for them and put their careers as missionaries ahead of being with their children. I know a lot of them resented this—I never did. I never doubted my parents' love for me. It always was, 'This is the way it is.'"

I'm not sure that's altogether true, but my mother must have needed to believe it. By denying a sense of abandonment she invented for herself a coping strategy and equilibrium. Winifred, on the other hand, didn't deny anything: "I felt I didn't know Mother and Dad and they didn't know me," she said. "And when they came back [from Africa] it was almost like meeting strangers. It took the entire summer to get acquainted, and then they were gone again. I just feel a loss."

———— · ————

A year after I filmed the *Return to Cameroun* interviews, Aunt Winifred told me she and Esther would be joining a Presbyterian Church-sponsored tour of Cameroun in December 1989. I loved the prospect of seeing the country and gathering material for the movie, so I booked passage for myself and San Francisco videographer Fawn Yacker. In retrospect, I'm awed at the pluck of my aunts, joining a trip of that size at seventy-two and sixty-nine. We flew from Paris to Douala, Cameroun, on Air France, then survived an Air Cameroun flight to the capital Yaounde on a rickety plane with overhead compartments that flapped open during takeoff and seats that shook because they weren't properly bolted to the floor.

From Yaounde we traveled overland by bus to the villages where the Presbyterian Church established missions in the early twentieth century: Kribi, Sakbayeme, Lolodorf, and especially Elat, where my mother and aunts were born. In each village we were treated like VIPs and greeted with long receiving lines that sometimes stretched 500 yards. Beaming with excitement, Esther and Winifred surprised themselves by drawing forth a few Bulu phrases ("Mbolo" means Hello, "Akeva" means Thank

Esther, Winifred and I at the Douala, Cameroun airport.

Esther and Winifred with Jean-Samuel Eba Ela, a resident of Elat who fifty years prior had been my grandfather's secretary at the Frank James Industrial School.

you) and chatting with their animated hosts. It was their first time in Cameroun since 1931.

People danced, sang, played drums. In Elat we were given a special concert inside the old brick church my grandfather built. Five choirs sang, each one more lustrous and amazing than the one before. There was great food: lots of plantains and bananas and yams, plus the mysterious "bush meat"—a term for any animal, species unspecified, that was killed in the wild. We met village elders who had known my grandparents and remembered the Hope sisters as little girls. One Bulu grandmother got teary when she spoke of meeting my grandfather in her early years. She called him "notre pere" (our father).

Travel reveals a lot about people, and for two-and-a-half weeks I got to appreciate how different Esther and Winifred really were. Both had lived in Cincinnati for decades, raised families there and in later years became expert crafters of miniaturist houses, working side-by-side in a studio in Esther's home. They looked alike, both short and white-haired. They dressed alike and had a rapport and common language you see in sisters and lifelong best friends.

Yet, while Esther had an easy laugh and roll-with-the-punches demeanor, Winifred was easily unsettled by the delays and frustrations of travel. In the bus, she chattered nervously and described, along with comforting memories, a host of long-ago slights she suffered as a child. At the mention of Cameron Love, a missionary kid with whom she was often paired because of their age, Winifred cringed. "I couldn't *stand* Cameron Love!" she exclaimed. It was as if the distant past in all its wounds and injustices was entirely accessible to her, and as if, by talking about it, she was experiencing the emotions anew.

At one point in Cameroun, Winifred started to believe she'd contracted malaria. (She hadn't.) And since our accommodations were hardly posh, she became fixated on the quality of bathroom facilities and described them in her travel journal. I'm slightly older now than she was then, and I totally get that concern. Winifred could carry on, but I marveled when someone in our tour group groused about the "dirty" feminists in the States and Winifred quickly reminded her of the freedoms she enjoyed thanks to feminists. I loved Winifred and ultimately grew closer to her than to Esther, who, for all her cheer and easy laughter, was more guarded with her emotions.

———— ✦ ————

Winifred's daughter Linda also grew up hearing Africa stories, and in March 2013 she took her mom to Chicago to see Bushman at the Field Museum of Natural History, where he'd been taxidermied and made a permanent exhibit. Bushman died in

1951, but Chicago still remembered him. Linda wanted to give her mom something special—"a last hurrah," she called it—so she rented a van and drove from Cincinnati with her mother Winifred, daughter Selita and granddaughter Nevaeh. Four generations.

Linda contacted the Lincoln Park Zoo and Field Museum in advance, and officials at both places were thrilled to hear from her. On a drizzly March afternoon, zoo representatives warmly received Winifred and her family. I was there, too. The zoo's primatologist and historian spoke to us, as well as a reporter from the *Chicago Sun-Times* and a videographer from the museum.

The next day at the Field Museum, a publicist staged a media moment when Winifred was wheeled up to the large plexiglass cube enclosing Bushman. There were photographers and more reporters. Winifred and Bushman were covered in all the Chicago papers ("He was my sweet little boy," she told the *Chicago Tribune*), and the story was picked up by the Huffington Post and London's *Daily Mail*. "Hello, old friend!" read the *Daily Mail* headline. "Ninety-two-year-old woman visits the gorilla she cared for as a girl living in Africa (but he's a little stiffer this time around)."

Museum aficionados, staff and volunteers treated Winifred, in her wheelchair and portable oxygen concentrator, like a bonafide celebrity. Several old-timers remembered Bushman from their childhood in Chicago, when he was still alive. The museum director made a presentation, and afterward volunteers and several museum employees met in a private room, where I showed *Return to Cameroun* and Winifred answered questions about her friendship with baby Bushman.

Winifred got a huge lift from the Chicago festivities. We all did. No doubt it was tiring for her, but the attention made Winifred feel special and gave her a warm glow. It was validation that her early life had been exceptional and in a small way linked to history.

Winifred at the Bushman display in Chicago's Field Museum of Natural History, with her great-granddaughter Nevaeh, 2013. *Photo courtesy of Chicago History Museum.*

She went home to Cincinnati and then, like a scene from a movie or a nineteenth-century novel, she died eighteen days later.

Today the Bushman display at the Field Museum commemorates Winifred's visit with one photo of her visiting the museum in 2013 and another of her holding baby Bushman in Cameroun eighty-two years earlier.

I wish my mother Roberta and Aunt Esther had been part of the celebration in Chicago, since they also knew Bushman in Africa. But I'm grateful that Winifred, who for so long felt overlooked as the youngest child, had a joyous experience shortly before death. I like to think she passed with a sweet cloud of memory enveloping her. The sound of rain on the thatch roof of her childhood African home. Her father's robust laughter. Cicadas singing in the grass on warm evenings. Baby Bushman in her arms or tugging at her leg.

Epilogue

At the turn of the 19th century, French novelist and literary critic Marcel Proust popularized a set of questions that he believed would reveal a person's true nature. The questionnaire was later adapted by French talk show host Bernard Pivot and appeared for many years on the back page of *Vanity Fair* magazine.

I've appropriated and expanded a bit on the Proust Questionnaire, asking and answering each question.

What is your idea of perfect happiness? A world without war, famine, bigotry or Trump. **What is your greatest fear?** Environmental collapse. **What is your most marked characteristic?** Curiosity. **What is the trait you most admire in others?** Kindness.

What is the trait you most deplore in yourself? Procrastination. **What is the trait you most deplore in others?** Deliberate cruelty. **What is your greatest extravagance?** Travel. **What do you consider the most overrated virtue?** Frugality. **On what occasion do you lie?** To spare someone from an uncomfortable truth they're better off not knowing.

What do you dislike about your appearance? An expanding waistline. **Which word or phrase do you most overuse?** "Oy." **If you could change one thing about yourself, what would it be?** I would be more patient, less critical.

What living person do you most admire? Jane Goodall, with Dolly Parton a close second. **What person not living do you most admire?** Abraham Lincoln, Congressman John Lewis, Nelson Mandela, Elizabeth Taylor, Robert F. Kennedy Sr.

What is your favorite sound? Babies laughing. **Your least favorite sound?** The shrill, insistent beep when a delivery truck goes in reverse. **What is your favorite word?** Yes. **What is your least favorite word?** Iconic. **What profession other than your own would you like to attempt?** Photography. **What profession other than your own would you not like to attempt?** Coal mining.

When and where were you happiest? Immersed in a creative project. **Which talent would you most like to have?** To sing really well and play piano. **What do you consider your greatest achievement?** Not losing my curiosity. **If you were to die and come back as a person or thing, what would it be?** A Labrador Retriever.

What is your most treasured possession? Family photos. **Who is your favorite hero of fiction?** Huckleberry Finn or Atticus Finch. **Where would you like to live?** Where I am now, but if I had tons of money I'd buy a second home in Manhattan with a view of Central Park. **Who are your heroes in real life?** Advocates for justice, humanitarian aid workers, animal rescue volunteers.

How would you like to die? Swiftly, quietly. **If you're buried, what do you want your gravestone to say?** "Tell me a story."

If Heaven exists, what would you like to hear God say when you arrive at the Pearly Gates? "You didn't do too badly, but I'm sending you back for another go. Have more fun this time; lead with kindness."

What word best captures the spirit of this book and the impetus to write it? Gratitude.

Acknowledgments

When she won her Oscar in 1982, actress Maureen Stapleton said, "I want to thank everybody I ever met in my entire life." I don't want to go quite that far, but to the friends and colleagues who gave me their time and encouragement during the writing of this book I offer my heartfelt thanks.

Regan McMahon was a stalwart and enthusiastic partisan. A fine editor and "grammarian extraordinaire," as her husband Blair Jackson once noted, Regan generously read several versions of the text and provided careful counsel up to the very last stages of production.

Eagle-eyed pro Cynthia Rubin did a thoughtful and meticulous line edit in the book's early stages, and three years later did the final proofread. Rob Jerome, a friend for more than 50 years, read a late draft of the book and made important suggestions.

Thanks to Carol Gould and Guy Albert for warm and steady support over the years. Along with Risa Nye, Stephen Silha, David Tuttle and Kevin Vandehey, they listened as I read parts of the book out loud — a helpful exercise for any writer.

Thanks to John Zussman and the *MyRetrospect* team, past and present, for creating and sustaining a forum in which I could write and remember.

Acknowledgments

Thanks to book designer Ashley Ingram for her creativity, enthusiasm and discerning eye.

Thanks to my brother Dave, the only other surviving member of my immediate family, for digitizing hundreds of old family photos and for help in remembering early family history.

About the Author

Edward Guthmann is a journalist and author of the memoir *Wild Seed: Searching for My Brother Dan.* He was a staff writer and film critic at the *San Francisco Chronicle* for twenty-five years, where his writing won accolades from the California Newspaper Publishers Assn., San Francisco Cable Car Awards, and the American Society of Feature and Sunday Editors. Also a filmmaker, he directed the documentary *Return to Cameroun* and its companion piece, *Journey to Cameroun.* He lives in Oakland. www.edwardguthmann.com